Wait! Don't Move to Canada!

A Stay-and-Fight Strategy to Win Back America

Bill Scher
Executive Editor of LiberalOasis.com

with a Foreword by
Janeane Garofalo and Sam Seder

RODALE

For Gina-Louise, Snow White of the Left

My partner, my editor, my love

Printed in the United States of America
Rodale Inc. makes every effort to use acid-free ♾, recycled paper ♻.

Cover design by Joanna Williams
Cover illustration by Bruce MacPherson
Interior design by Gavin Robinson

Library of Congress Cataloging-in-Publication Data

Scher, Bill.
    Wait! don't move to Canada! : a stay-and-fight strategy to win back
America / Bill Scher   foreword by Janeane Garofalo and Sam Seder.
      p.   cm.
    Includes bibliographical references.
    ISBN 13 978–1–59486–396–7 paperback
    ISBN 10 1–59486–396–2 paperback
    1. Liberalism—United States.   2. United States—Politics and govern-
ment, date I. Title.
    JC574.2.U6S34   2006
    320.51'30973—dc22   2006014437

Distributed to the trade by Holtzbrinck Publishers

2 4 6 8 10 9 7 5 3 1   paperback

We inspire and enable people to improve their lives and the world around them
For more of our products visit **rodalestore.com** or call 800-848-4735

"Liberalism properly understood is not just consistent with the American idea. Liberalism properly understood *is* the American idea."

—MARIO CUOMO

CONTENTS

FOREWORD

By Janeane Garofalo and Sam Seder

Moving to Canada isn't for everyone. It's a relatively drastic step, as Bill's pithy title suggests; everyone knows it's a lot colder up there. A. Lot. Colder. Plus, the most famous band to come out of Canada is Rush. Seriously, Canada, Rush?[1]

Although, to be fair, isn't the health care much better up there? Don't some people speak French? We think that would actually be kind of enjoyable: a little cultural and linguistic diversity for a change. George Bush, certainly, wouldn't be caught vacationing north of the border. Frankly, after some more thought, we probably would have preferred Bill title his book *Please Don't Wait: Move to Canada Before Alberto Gonzales Extraordinarily Renders Your Ass to Libya*. But instead

---

[1] The flippant tone Sam uses to mask his unrequited love for Canada is a little embarrassing. Sam not only loves Rush, the Barenaked Ladies, SCTV, Mike Myers, and the Royal Mountees--or is it Mounties (Dudley Dooright, et al.)? Anyway. Sam has been in love with Canada for more than 17 years. It started out innocently enough in 1979, when his Yeshiva sponsored a Great White North Dad-n-Lad ski trip. Seder Sr. (Sam's father) never enjoyed his son's company. Therefore, Canada became Sam's closest companion and confidante. As it turned out, Canada was just being nice. Canada is nice to everyone. Sam, as usual, thought he was special. Young Seder was besotted and much too fat for his height (but that's a whole other story... available at Amazon.com). Canada just wanted to be friends, and would only return Sam's phone calls sporadically. Canada's failure to find Sam attractive has had a profound effect on his record collection, and his psyche... hence, the aforementioned "flippant tone." -JG

Bill insisted that because he wrote it, this is technically "his book," and it's "really not our job" to "grossly intrude on his work" and "act like we know everything just because we have a national radio show." Fine then. When the Air America stretch Cadillac Escalade (with the Majority Report logo stenciled on the roof) doesn't pick you up next week to bring you to the studio, don't blame us, Bill, don't blame us.

In truth, the possibility of moving to Canada after another George W. Bush "election" "win" hasn't totally escaped us. Clearly, life in America today is increasingly tough for a liberal. The rights of corporations expand while the rights of individual people contract. Purveyors of dogmatic religious doctrine undermine hard science. Those of us simply looking for things like quality health care for our families not underwritten by Vioxx or Viagra and a creationism-free science curriculum for our children are out of luck for the time being. Waving the Maple Leaf flag, as it were, looks more and more appealing.

But as liberals, much to our own chagrin, we're stuck with one nagging obligation that the fringe fundamentalists and crony corporatists lack: We care about others.

Yes, true, that sounds slightly wimpy. But it's not. Really.

Look, it would be a lot easier to cut-and-run to Canada, but we all have an obligation not to, an obligation to stay and fight those who want to turn our country into a playground for the selfish and self-righteous.

Why won't we move to Canada, besides the weather and music? Simple: Because there are some people who can't.

This would all be different if Tom DeLay and Pat Robertson wanted to formally annex Colorado Springs and move all the right-wingers there to live their own solitary, celibate lives of brand-name bliss for all eternity. That would be just swell, because they wouldn't be forcing their corruptive wishes on the rest of us.

But that's not at all what they want.

The conservative cabal doesn't want to live alone. No, they want to make money off working people who can barely afford immunizations for their children, let alone health care or, heaven forbid, a vacation. These right-wingers want to force their fundamentalist laws on the bodies of all women, not just on their wives and family members. They want to end affirmative action nationally, slash taxes for the ultra-wealthy, and gut the secure retirement accounts of working people.

Again, this would all be just peachy if all the rest of us could (or wanted to) just pack the bags and move. But we all can't, and we don't really want to. We like this country.

The liberals of this country have always stood at the forefront of social progress in America. The legacy of leaders like Susan B. Anthony, Robert La Follette, Franklin Delano Roosevelt, and Rev. Martin Luther King, Jr., shows that liberalism has brought about almost all of our social advancements.

The work we face isn't easy, glorious, or even necessarily obvious. Politics and activism can seem daunting unless you have no real job and all day to read the news like.... uh ... we do. Behind every sweeping movement and every great orator or leader are teams of people doing the homework and analysis. Those who have been faithful readers of Bill's blog, LiberalOasis.com, know that his political judgment is invaluable, post after post. And as liberal politics become more democratized, as more and more individual liberals are educated and empowered politically through the Internet and liberal talk-radio, we're happy people that like Bill are around to give us the backstory, to do our opposition research, and to work as our field guide.

Besides, let's face it: None of us were really going to move to Canada anyway.[2]

---

[2] Sam was.—JG

INTRODUCTION

IT'S ALL ABOUT THE PRINCIPLES

The day after Bill Clinton beat George H. W. Bush decisively to take the White House in 1992, the Republican Senate Minority Leader Bob Dole held a press conference, and the first thing out of his mouth was:

> *57 percent of the Americans who voted in the presidential election voted against Bill Clinton, and I intend to represent that majority on the floor of the US Senate.*

He finished his remarks with:

> *I think [Clinton] got some good news and some bad news last night.... The good news is that he's getting a honeymoon in Washington. The bad news is that Bob Dole is going to be chaperone.*

Dole's message was that Republicans were unbowed, defiant, ready to get back in the ring and fight.

Compare that to how the Democrats handled their defeat in 2004. House Minority Leader Nancy Pelosi offered the following: "House Democrats stand ready to work with the President. Despite our divisions, there are many places where we should be able to agree." Then senator-elect Barack Obama said, "We all have a stake in seeing him [George W. Bush] have a successful presidency. I don't think that the Democrats succeed by rooting against the president in office."

The Dems' message: conciliatory, timid, showing no inclination to fight at all.

This is not a difference of personality types. The difference is one of principles. The Republican Party has them. The Democratic Party doesn't.

WHY I DIDN'T MOVE TO CANADA AND YOU DIDN'T EITHER

Liberals may joke about fleeing to Canada or Europe when the right wing wins on Election Day, but a scant few actually do. This is not just because no one likes to pack. It's because we love America and its ideals too much to simply walk away from it.

Yet we do joke, because sometimes the situation feels hopeless—especially at those times when we look to the Democratic Party to fight for our principles and we fail to see much fight. This can lead us to consider abandoning the Democratic Party altogether to start a third party, although the reality is that it's easier to reform an existing party than to start a party from scratch. (See Party, Green; Party, Reform; and Party, Libertarian.)

The Democratic Party can be reformed and win national elections again—once it is understood and accepted that liberal principles are the path to victory, not the obstacle to it. And once you, dear reader, do your part. That's the mission of this book: to share with you a winning strategy so you can help forge a long-term Democratic majority, usher in a new era of American liberalism, and banish the thought of moving to Canada forever.

SINCE YOU'RE STAYING, YOU MIGHT AS WELL FIGHT

Liberal views are so often dismissed, distorted, and delegitimized by the mainstream media that many Democratic officeholders are reluctant to voice them. But complaining that politicians are afraid to lead won't change things. We must take matters into our own hands and provide that voice.

Fortunately, a new liberal infrastructure is forming that's giving us the ability to be heard. A big part of that is the burgeoning liberal blogosphere—the loose collection of Web logs (online journals, commonly referred to as "blogs") and other online communities.

Blogging didn't begin as a political phenomenon. But around 2002, frustration with the media's fawning coverage of the Bush Administration boiled over, prompting many liberals to flock to the Internet. Finally, no longer did we have to rely on professional pundits who were either hostile to liberalism or compelled to suppress their liberalism so that they might appear objective. We could do our own research, provide our own analysis, and instantly share it with other liberals across the country.

I was among that first wave of liberal bloggers, not having any sense at the time that I would be part of something revolutionary. I had a background in public relations, and since liberals have long struggled with how to succinctly communicate their beliefs in the age of the sound bite, I felt I had some expertise to share. After getting over being stunned that the Web address LiberalOasis.com was available, I put up a site there and began offering news analysis and strategic advice on a daily basis

I also ended up as a weekly commentator on the Air America talk radio show *The Majority Report* with Janeane Garofalo and Sam Seder. Janeane and Sam realized right away that there was a natural relationship between blogging and talk radio. Talk radio hosts are always hungry for fresh angles on news stories, and the blogosphere is essentially a volunteer army of passionate diggers. The two also saw there was a value in growing the blogosphere by encouraging their listeners to join in. They began booking bloggers on a regular basis, including two who had nurtured the largest online liberal communities: Markos Moulitsas of dailykos.com and Duncan Black of atrios.blogspot.com. And me, apparently because they liked my stuff.

So, though we've come a long way, the real fight is just beginning. The Air America community and the blogosphere have grown fast—Air America has more than 3 million weekly listeners, and DailyKos.com attracts about 600,000 daily visits. But in a country of 300 million, that's just a good start. We need more people like you blogging, listening, calling, and talking about the key issues to fully reinvigorate the liberal grassroots.

We liberals also need to take stock of why we've been losing and they've been winning. The first order of business, then, is getting to the bottom of what Republicans are doing right and Democrats are doing wrong.

"PRINCIPLED" REPUBLICANS VERSUS RUDDERLESS DEMOCRATS

I said that the Republican Party has principles and the Democrats don't. Don't misunderstand me. I'm not suggesting that Howard Dean is less noble than Tom DeLay. As a general rule, individual Democratic politicians are far more upstanding than Republican ones. But the Republican *Party* has articulated a clear set of principles that they do not waver from, and the Democratic Party hasn't.

Win or lose, the GOP talks about three core principles: less government, lower taxes, and a strong military. It doesn't matter that when in charge, Republican politicians have been known to grow government, raise taxes, and stretch the military too thin. Party leaders have decided that less government, lower taxes, and a strong military is what they stand for and what they run on. That's their story, and they're sticking with it for good reason—because more often than not, it has helped them win.

When they do lose, Republicans don't devolve into making soul-searching spectacles of themselves. There's no debate about whether they still support lower taxes or if they should finally give peace a chance. They have their factions and their squabbles, but the big-picture stuff is set in stone. Right after any election, they can get down to the business of dismantling our government at home and provoking conflict abroad.

Not so for the Democrats. There is no clear consensus within the Democratic Party on how to address fundamental policy matters such as the role of government, the ideal level of taxation, and the proper direction for our foreign policy, not to mention how to approach hot-button social issues such as abortion and gay rights. And that makes it hard to be defiant in the face of defeat. How can you confidently jump back into the fray if you can't be sure that your buddies have your back? If Democrats clearly and consistently articulated a set of principles, and if they supported those principles in good times *and* bad, people would know what they were fighting for and be willing to fight that much harder.

Following the 2004 losses, instead of showing steadfast support for bedrock beliefs, Democratic leaders like Pelosi and Obama tried to position the party as being opposed to confrontation and support-ive of compromise. In theory, that sounds admirable enough—put-ting aside political differences for the good of the country. But in reality, Democrats have looked weak, and the country has suffered.

Coming up with a few general-purpose, inoffensive buzzwords won't help the Democratic Party regain the trust of the public. Buzz-words can't explain the profound differences in how the two parties govern. They don't give voters a meaty reason to throw one party out of power and choose the other.

No, a party of the people, by the people, and for the people can't get away with hiding *from* the people its ideology.

And we shouldn't have to move to Canada to celebrate ours.

EMBRACE THE L-WORD AND WIN THE CENTER

"Call me a conservative. . . . I'm proud of it. I vote that way. . . . Is there anybody in the Senate who will admit to being liberal?"
—Senator Lindsey Graham (R-SC)

You probably see yourself as independent-minded. Being part of a clique, going along with the crowd, might have had some appeal in high school. But by the time most of us are adults, we are perfectly happy thinking for ourselves.

This is proven out in politics. For years, the Harris poll has asked Americans whether they consider themselves liberal, conservative, or moderate. The nonideological "moderate" always wins. In 2005, moderates were at 42 percent, conservatives 34, and liberals 20. Those numbers have held pretty steady over the past 25 years.

Yet Republican politicians don't flinch from the term *conservative*, even though conservatives are a minority. They've figured out that whatever risks the label carries, it's even more risky to be perceived as standing for nothing. And so they strive to define conservatism in a way that extends its appeal to nonconservatives. George W. Bush's "compassionate conservatism" is one example. This strategy helps Republicans not only win elections, but also claim mandates to move the country in their preferred direction.

This is not how the Democratic Party has approached politics for some time, because it refuses to come to terms with its ideological foundation: liberalism. Until it does, it won't win many national elections and won't influence the direction of the country. Sure, now and then charismatic figures such as Bill Clinton might come along who can work short-term political magic. And yes, backlashes against the party in power, as during Watergate or the economic recession of the early 1990s, can result in temporary political gains. But without securing mandates to move the country in a different direction, such victories will be fleeting. They won't stop the right-wing tide that is eroding the foundations of our country and worsening the quality of life of Americans, not to mention citizens around the globe.

But if only 20 percent of the country considers itself liberal, is a public embrace of liberalism political suicide? Well, that percentage only indicates people's reaction to the liberal *label*, not to liberal policies. In fact, polls have shown:

- More than 75 percent of Americans say that the government should be responsible for guaranteeing health care for all and making sure no one lives in poverty.
- 60 percent say that they believe spending on infrastructure improvements is better for the country's economy than tax cuts.
- 63 percent say that gays should be allowed to serve openly in the military; 60 percent support either marriage or civil unions for gays.

- 61 percent believe that the president should nominate Supreme Court justices who will uphold Roe v. Wade.

Clearly, you don't have to call yourself a liberal to hold liberal views.

So just how did *liberal* become such a bad word? The short answer is: We liberals let it.

A QUICK HISTORY OF THE L-WORD

Democrats didn't always run from the liberal label. On September 14, 1960, John F. Kennedy formally accepted the nomination for president from the New York Liberal Party with a speech that began:

> *What do our opponents mean when they apply to us the label "liberal"? If by "liberal" they mean, as they want people to believe, someone who is soft in his policies abroad, who is against local government, and who is unconcerned with the taxpayer's dollar, then the record of this party and its members demonstrate that we are not that kind of liberal.*
>
> *But if by a liberal they mean someone who looks ahead and not behind, someone who welcomes new ideas without rigid reactions, someone who cares about the welfare of the people—their health, their housing, their schools, their jobs, their civil rights, and their civil liberties—someone who believes we can break through the stalemate and suspicions that grip us in our policies abroad, if that is what they mean by a liberal, then I'm proud to say I'm a liberal.*

It was not ideal for Kennedy to essentially say that there are good liberals and bad liberals, but he did make an attempt to positively define the term instead of rejecting it. That strategy was ditched after George McGovern's landslide loss of 1972, which was unfairly attributed to McGovern's liberal platform. Richard Nixon, in many ways a moderate pragmatist, had approval ratings that were solidly above 50 percent through almost all of the election year, making him tough to beat regardless of opponent. And McGovern himself proved to be not exactly ready for primetime. He presided over a chaotic, mismanaged convention where his acceptance speech was delivered at 3:00 A.M., and his pick for vice-president, Senator Thomas Eagleton, was revealed to have had electroshock therapy, sparking a media frenzy. McGovern initially said he stood by Eagleton "1,000 percent," only to dump him a few days later—a dramatic cave-in that undermined his credibility.

But liberalism was blamed, and in 1976 the party nominated the moderate Jimmy Carter, who eked out a victory over an unpopular Gerald Ford. In 1980, Carter was renominated after beating back a primary challenge from Ted Kennedy by running ads calling Kennedy "too liberal." Yet when Carter lost his bid for a second term to Ronald Reagan, liberalism was blamed again.

The 1984 Democratic nominee, Walter Mondale, is often considered a liberal, but that's not how he ran. He painted himself as a pragmatist and ran under the banner of the New Realism. After his nominating convention, the *New York Times* reporter Warren Weaver noted the shift:

> *The Democratic Party has moved away from some hallmarks of its tradition of liberalism in the 8 years since Walter F. Mondale's first national campaign.... What may*

be the only overt mention of liberalism in the 1984 platform maintains that the answer to crime is "neither a permissive liberalism nor a static conservatism."

Oddly enough, despite the Democratic fear of the word, Republicans had not used *liberal* as a main attack line prior to 1988. Ronald Reagan didn't use the term against Jimmy Carter at the 1980 Republican Convention or during their lone debate. At the 1984 convention, Reagan did criticize Mondale's New Realism as the "Old Liberalism," but again, he did not utter the word during the debates.

The year 1988 was a different matter. That presidential campaign became the watershed moment that turned the word into the all-purpose slur it is today. George H. W. Bush's entire strategy to reverse a 17-point deficit in the polls rested on slapping the Scarlet L on Michael Dukakis and the "liberal Democrat Congress." He used the word so much in one of the debates that Dukakis responded in frustration, "I think Mr. Bush has used the label 'liberal' at least 10 times."

Throughout the campaign, Dukakis had tried to avoid the moniker. At times he called himself a conservative, pointing to his fiscal record as governor. He famously, and wrongly, said in his nomination acceptance speech that the election would be about "competence," not "ideology." In a particularly awkward exchange with ABC News's Ted Koppel late in the campaign, he struggled to answer the question, "What is a liberal in 1988?" During the exchange, he made the mushy proclamation: "I think all of us have combinations of liberal and conservative about us, Ted. I'm not a liberal."

However, just 5 days later, with 9 days left to go in the campaign, down by double digits in the polls, he threw a proverbial long ball.

Speaking to a cheering throng during a whistle-stop train tour, Dukakis announced:

> *Yes, I am a liberal, in the tradition of Franklin Roosevelt and Harry Truman and John Kennedy. . . . I'm not going to let the Republican Party pervert that word or give it a meaning it doesn't have.*

It was a sloppy reversal, yet ending the evasion helped the campaign gain traction. By Election Day, the gap in Gallup's daily tracking poll had narrowed by 8 points, and Dukakis's favorable rating had risen 7 points. Obviously, it was too little too late, but the strong finish provided some evidence that a proud embrace of liberalism could help and not hurt.

That was not the lesson Democrats learned. More than ever before, the liberal label was shunned.

THE LIMITS OF CLINTON'S CHARISMA

So, Bill Clinton was not doing something novel by running away from liberalism in 1992 by offering a "third way" that was "not conservative or liberal . . . not even Republican or Democratic." He was merely refining an approach that every Democratic presidential candidate over the last 16 years had tried.

Clinton faced an unpopular incumbent mired in a sluggish economy. And Clinton had far more charisma than your typical pol. So he won.

But what did he actually win? He didn't bring with him much of an ideological mandate because he didn't run on one. He had a mandate to reform welfare and pass a "middle-class tax cut," but little else. When he proposed government solutions to problems, it didn't matter that they weren't "big government" solutions. He was slapped with the "liberal" slur anyway, and the slurs worked. His main initiatives, on economic stimulus and health care, were blocked. His deficit-reduction plan—which involved raising taxes, something on which he did not campaign—passed with no GOP support and considerable GOP criticism. In turn, he lost Democratic control of Congress 2 years after being elected.

Clinton was forced to play a defensive role for the rest of his tenure, staving off some right-wing proposals and accommodating on others, which he did brilliantly. He is unquestionably a master at personal political survival. But by the end of his two terms, he had not left the party with any sort of ideological direction beyond "We're not as crazy as Newt Gingrich," who's not even in Congress anymore. This is in stark contrast to Ronald Reagan, who left Republicans with an antigovernment philosophy that still serves as the bedrock of the party today.

THE NECESSITY OF REVITALIZING THE TERM *LIBERAL*

Okay, so it's better for our long-term prospects if we embrace liberalism. But why sweat the word itself? If so few people currently like the term *liberal*, if it alienates moderates and independents, why not repackage liberal ideas and philosophy under a new brand name?

Because Democrats and liberals have tried it before, ditching the word and calling themselves *progressive* instead. Thirty years after McGovern, no Democratic leader has defended the word *liberal* (outside of Dukakis, whose defense only lasted 9 days). Even when the most liberal members of the House of Representatives created a caucus to influence the direction of the Democrats, they called it the Progressive Caucus, while its Republican counterpart, the Republican Study Committee, brags on its Web site that it's the "House's only conservative caucus."

The song and dance hasn't worked. The words *liberal* and *conservative* are too embedded in our lexicon. Those words will continue to be used to characterize where ideas and politicians stand on the political spectrum, whether we like it or not. Which makes abandoning *liberal* extremely dangerous. If one side is demonizing it, and the other side is ignoring it, it will be demonized.

Since conservatives are not ones to prematurely stop a good beating, they're continuing to pound away, making our situation worse. In 2004 we began to see the GOP meld the "flip-flop" slur with the "liberal" slur, giving *liberal* a brand new negative connotation. The slur used to just indicate someone who is "outside the mainstream," who "doesn't share your values." Now it is starting to mean someone you can't trust, someone who refuses to be honest about his or her position. Deliberately ducking the label plays into this strategy. It only confirms such suspicions and makes it harder to win over voters than would consistently defining the label on our own terms.

DON'T WAIT FOR A SAVIOR

What we can't do is sit back and wait for a charismatic leader to do this job for us. Most politicians, even the charismatic ones, are followers, not visionaries. As far as many Democratic Party leaders are concerned, the Clinton way has worked and the liberal way has not. They won't try anything dramatically different until they see with their own two eyes that an embrace of liberal principles is resonating with the public. That means people who are not in the party leadership have to step up—people like you and me.

Fortunately, in part because of the blossoming blogosphere, the Democratic Party is becoming increasingly decentralized, fueled more by small donors than corporate donors, interacting more with the grassroots and less with Beltway political consultants. If we do a better job articulating Democratic principles than the Washington Democrats do, and we can prove that our approach is showing signs of resonating with the public, the politicians will ride our wave.

But we're not close to where the Republican Party is on this score. Despite its more top-down structure, the GOP manages to maintain a more stable relationship with the members of its conservative base. It does not lurch to the right in its primaries and lurch back to the middle for general elections. On an ongoing basis, conservatives offer right-wing ideas along with pragmatic strategies. In turn, politicians listen. It's not a flawless relationship. Sometimes disagreements between Republicans and their leadership spill out into the open, but the relationship is strong enough to withstand the friction.

Democratic politicians would be far more willing to cultivate that kind of relationship if the percentage of people willing to call themselves liberal were closer to 34 percent than 20 percent. It's up to us to fix that. It's up to us—whether you presently see yourself as a liberal, moderate, independent, progressive, Democrat, or disillusioned Republican—to scrub off the stigma and define liberalism for today. It's up to us to stop letting the right wing tell the world what our principles are and start doing it ourselves.

STAY AND FIGHT

Embrace the L-Word and Win the Center

✓Become an Air America listener and supporter. If it's not on the air in your town, you can hear it on satellite radio or stream it on your computer by logging on to www.airamericaradio. com. Or, better yet, organize a petition effort to get a local station with weak ratings to become an Air America affiliate. When station owners realize that there's a liberal audience out there, they just may try to serve it.

✓Join the blogosphere. A good place to start is my own site, www.LiberalOasis.com, which is loaded with links to other leading liberal blogs and Web sites. The bigger the liberal blogosphere is, the more influence we will have on the nation's political discourse. (More on blogs, and how to start one, in Chapter 10.) And, I invite you to wear your liberalism proudly by purchasing some fine LiberalOasis gear; half of the profits go to antisweatshop organizations.

✓Be a proud liberal voice in your hometown. Write letters to your local newspaper and call in to local talk radio shows. Make a single point in 150 words or less. Don't feel like you have to fight every liberal battle every time out. You can always write another letter or make another call tomorrow or next week.

✓Connect with other liberals in your area by joining a chapter of Drinking Liberally (www.drinkingliberally.org), a nationwide network of informal weekly gatherings where liberals meet, chat, and drink. If there isn't a chapter in your area, start one.

✓Engage your elected representatives. Tell Democratic officials that taking liberal positions will strengthen the party and help them get re-elected. You can get contact information for your representatives at www.house.gov and www.senate.gov. Because of September 11, mail is delivered more slowly these days, so it's safer and quicker to use phone calls and faxes.

✓Town halls are a great way to engage your representatives directly. Contact their offices and get on their mailing lists so you'll know when such events are happening.

✓In all of your communications, label your views as "liberal," comfortably and confidently. Don't marginalize yourself by, for example, characterizing your opinions as "dissent." Dissenters are in the minority. Our goal is to be the majority.

CHAPTER 2

PROMOTE THE THREE R'S OF LIBERAL GOVERNMENT

They want the federal government controlling the Social Security, like it's some kind of federal program.

—George W. Bush

Everyone knows that Americans don't like government solutions to problems. Right? Well, these numbers from noted pollsters Stan and Anna Greenberg may surprise you. In 2003 they asked 1,000 likely voters what government should be responsible for. Here are some of the responses. Percentages combine those saying "strongly responsible" and "somewhat responsible":

- Protecting the environment: 93 percent (69 percent strongly)
- Keeping tabs on and regulating big corporations and powerful individuals who may abuse their position and hurt others in society: 92 percent (71 percent strongly)

- Ensuring equal opportunity for everyone: 88 percent (67 percent strongly)
- Guaranteeing a quality public education: 87 percent (70 percent strongly)
- Guaranteeing that all have health care insurance: 79 percent (60 percent strongly)
- Making sure that no one lives in poverty: 76 percent (49 percent strongly)
- Helping people not fall back when they face a crisis, become unemployed, or face big health care, college, or retirement costs: 75 percent (40 percent strongly)

A bunch of communist subversives, those Americans.

Actually, what these figures show is that the historic bedrock principle of the Democratic Party—the belief in the power of representative government to respond to public concerns and responsibly manage our resources—is still in sync with the sensibilities of the vast majority of us.

Yet that's not a principle you hear Democrats pledging allegiance to these days. They feel that they lost the White House to Ronald Reagan in 1980, and the Congress to Newt Gingrich in 1994, for being perceived as the party of big government, and now they don't even want to go near there. And so you'll hear Democrats brag that Bill Clinton cut the size of the federal government in 1990s; during the 2004 presidential campaign, John Kerry said his health care proposal was "not a government plan"; and in their 2004 platform, the party asserted that they "believe the private sector, not government, is the engine of economic growth and job creation."

The point here is not that these stances and actions were necessarily wrong. It's that they were wrongly framed in a defensive, antigovernment way. By bending over backward to insist that they are wary of government solutions, Democrats have inadvertently signaled that they might agree with Republicans about the role of government—or worse, that they are insincerely pretending to agree because they think that's what the public wants to hear. That makes it harder for Democrats to advocate for a representative, responsive, and responsible government that can effectively meet our wants and needs.

REFRAMING THE DEBATE: NOT BIG VERSUS SMALL

One major fallacy is that people want small government for its own sake. In the Greenberg poll, people were asked what they disliked about paying taxes. Only 22 percent said it was because "the government doesn't do anything for me." A whopping 65 percent agreed that it was because "the government is too wasteful and inefficient" (39 percent agreed strongly). Taken together with the poll numbers, which clearly show a desire for government to tackle major societal problems, we see a cry for *better* government, not necessarily *less* government.

Since Republicans can't win by arguing that government should do less, they instead play on the public skepticism about the effectiveness of our government in order to demonize it. The more people distrust government, the easier it is for Republicans to advance an antigovernment agenda.

The modern origin of this strategy was Ronald Reagan's successful presidential campaign against the Democratic incumbent Jimmy Carter. Reagan is known for saying in his first inaugural address, "Government is not the solution to our problem. Government is the problem." However, in his nomination acceptance speech, Reagan did not simplistically trash government. He connected his antigovernment beliefs to the public's desire for effective government:

I pledge to restore to the federal government the capacity to do the people's work without dominating their lives. I pledge to you a government that will not only work well, but wisely; its ability to act tempered by prudence and its willingness to do good balanced by the knowledge that government is never more dangerous than when our desire to have it help us blinds us to its great power to harm us.

As Carter's presidency was widely perceived as ineffective, people were open to a new approach that promised greater effectiveness. Reagan's suggestion that small government equals effective government stuck, and ever since then, the debate over the role of government has been framed in that way: small and effective versus big and ineffective. That framing makes losers out of Democrats. Republicans own "small," and Democrats, rightly, don't want anything to do with an Orwellian-sounding "big."

The goal for Democrats should be to reframe the debate so it is centered not on the size of our government but around the quality of our government. We should say that we want *representative* government that serves the public and brings people together, while Republicans want an *elitist* government that divides the nation and caters only to corporate donors and fringe fundamentalist religious leaders. We should say that Democrats want *responsive* government that does what the people ask of it, while Republicans want *callous* government that ignores people's concerns. We should say that Democrats want *responsible* government that wisely manages resources and forthrightly deals with problems, while Republicans have shown their belief in *reckless* government by running up massive debt and allowing social and environmental problems to worsen.

Representative, responsive, responsible—that should be our mantra. That is how Democrats will deliver the effective government that people desire.

CLINTON: TRAPPED IN THE GOP FRAME

When Bill Clinton famously said "the era of big government is over" in his 1996 State of the Union address, he was trying to reframe the debate so that Democrats could position themselves as standing for more effective government:

> *We know big government does not have all the answers. We know there's not a program for every problem. We have worked to give the American people a smaller, less bureaucratic government in Washington. And we have to give the American people one that lives within its means.*
>
> *The era of big government is over. But we cannot go back to the time when our citizens were left to fend for themselves. Instead, we must go forward as one America, one nation working together to meet the challenges we face together. Self-reliance and teamwork are not opposing virtues; we must have both.*
>
> *I believe our new, smaller government must work in an old-fashioned American way, together with all of our citizens through state and local governments, in the workplace, in religious, charitable and civic associations. Our goal must be to enable all our people to make the most of*

their own lives—with stronger families, more educational
opportunity, economic security, safer streets, a cleaner
environment in a safer world.

This is generally the right idea, but with one glaring problem. Clinton *equated* small government with effective government. Instead of recognizing that sometimes you need to cut and sometimes you need to grow, Clinton suggested that cutting is always right and growing is always wrong. That's exactly the Republican strategy, formulated by Reagan, to justify the termination of governmental responsibilities and stifle any discussion of taking on new ones. Clinton gets points for effort, but in the end, he didn't reframe the debate on liberal terms. He kept the debate on their terms.

RECONNECTING PEOPLE TO THEIR GOVERNMENT

Another Republican tactic is to portray "the government" as a distant and oppressive entity. George W. Bush promotes this idea with his signature line: "It's not the government's money. It's the people's money."

In 2000, Bush was less successful with his tack than Reagan was with his in 1980, as only Reagan won the popular vote. That is in large part because the public was not as upset with the effectiveness of the Clinton administration as it was with the Carter administration. Bush had less of an opening to exploit. Nevertheless, for the Republican Party to advance its antigovernment agenda, it must continue to foster notions of governmental ineffectiveness.

For example, look at how Bush weaves his pet soundbite into his pitch for Social Security privatization:

Today we have an opportunity to offer younger Americans a better deal than the current system. Today we can give every American the chance to tap into the power of compound interest, so they can get a higher rate of return on their money than the current system allows.

You might notice I said, "their money." See, we're not spending the government's money. The payroll taxes are the people's money. It's coming from hardworking people. . . .

Instead of sending all the payroll taxes to Washington, younger workers would be able to transfer part of their money directly into an account they own and that the government can never take away.

Bush tries to play on the public's skepticism of government effectiveness, saying that "Washington" can't make you as much money as you can yourself. But he's pushing more than just incompetence. Bush also describes an insidious "government" that wants to "take away" your money.

So while Republicans strive to disconnect people from their government, it is our job to counter that effort and rhetorically *reconnect* people to their government. How? Instead of characterizing government as "*the* government," like a cold, monstrous entity that tries to tell you what to do, whenever you get the chance, call it what it is: *our* government, an extension of ourselves, designed with liberal ideals in mind to pool and direct our collective resources for the greater good. Because it's not a choice between whether the government takes our money or we keep it. Our government's money is the people's money. And if we want our government to spend our money to improve the nation's health care system, to protect the environment, to strengthen our homeland security, to set aside land for national parks, and to eradicate poverty at home and abroad, then that's our choice.

HIGHLIGHTING EFFECTIVE GOVERNMENT

Still, rhetoric only goes so far in overcoming the main obstacle: people's skepticism of governmental effectiveness. We can fight that by playing up concrete examples where our government has worked.

An example of what *not* to do comes from former Democratic senator John Breaux. He shared this story on the Senate floor, recounting a run-in with a constituent who was concerned about Medicare:

> *I remember coming back home to New Orleans and having a lady come up to me in the airport and say, "You are all working on that health care reform back in Washington?" I said, "Yes, ma'am, we are."*
>
> *She said, "Whatever you do, don't let the federal government take over my Medicare."*

That's an interesting anecdote on its own. It shows how much people appreciate responsive and responsible government while also showing their lack of connection to it.

But perhaps more interesting is Breaux's response. Instead of saying to the constituent, "Boy! Isn't it something that this program, which provides such a good service, is actually managed by your federal government," Breaux chose to feed her misunderstanding of Medicare and her overall suspicion of government by saying, "Okay. We won't let that happen."

That was a missed opportunity on a small scale. In the Social Security battle of 2005, Democrats missed a far bigger opportunity. While they successfully blocked Bush's privatization plan by making

A Day Without Government in ConservativeLand
February 24, 2020
Dear Diary,
Sigh. Another Sunday shot to hell. Bunch of potholes opened up on the block, so me and the neighbors had to fill 'em. Everyone's on my case because all I have is the cheap asphalt. "You're bringing the whole block down!" they say. "Pine Street is laughing at us!" We'll see how they'll like it when their boss funnels their pension into his fourth summer home.

After feeling like an idiot out there, I get to feel like an idiot in front of my kid, trying to help him with his homework. Ever since Coca-Pepsi Cola took over the middle school, everyone's gotta know cola history backward and forward. What do I know about that? I thought everyone knew that in the 1800s the drink had a little cocaine in it, but he showed me in the textbook that that was some urban legend. See, I'm no help.

It looked like I'd finally get an hour to myself to watch some football, but then the power went out. Third time this year! At least the new Chinese power company that took over has been better than that British company. The Chinese take only 2 or 3 days to get things back up and running.

Before I knew it, it was time for my evening shift with the local militia to patrol the town borders. We're not going to let Piedmont swipe our coal stash again!

I was exhausted by the time I got home, but I thought I could at least have a romantic night with my wife. But I'm still having that...problem. She thinks it's a side-effect from my cholesterol pills, but I'm sure the drug maker would have mentioned on the label if something like that was possible.

It must be because I'm so tired all the time. If only the government didn't have so many people on Marriage Sanctity Patrol, maybe they could do some stuff around the neighborhood and I could catch a break! Oh, that's just me talking crazy again. I better get some rest. There's a busted traffic light to fix during tomorrow's lunch break....

the narrow case that Social Security is a good program and radical changes weren't necessary, they never articulated what Social Security's popularity says about the role of government. They never said that only with a representative government, responding to our needs and responsibly managing our resources could we have achieved the liberal goal of dignified retirement for all.

If Social Security privatization was ultimately defeated anyway, why does it matter that the moment was missed? Because when you use a victory on a single issue to make a broader argument about how your party would govern the country differently, you can fundamentally shift public opinion, set the stage for big election gains, and claim mandates for new policies.

That's how the Republicans, in 1994, ended 40 years of Democratic control of the House of Representatives and took over the entire Congress. As the '05 Democrats blocked Bush's plan to end guaranteed retirement insurance for every American, the '94 Republicans blocked Bill Clinton's plan to guarantee health insurance for every American. But the Republicans took their strategy a crucial step further. They understood that they weren't just trying to defeat a single proposal. They were trying to extinguish the public's desire for responsive government and sell their own antigovernment vision. The proof is in a key conservative strategy memo that counseled Republicans in Congress "to 'kill'—not amend—the Clinton plan" because if it passed it would "give Democrats a lock on the crucial middle class vote and revive the reputation of the party."

Just before Clinton put his health care vision to the nation in his 1994 State of the Union Address, then-Minority Whip Newt Gingrich framed the debate on his terms:

The President's plan was an effort on his part to convince the country that the government could run health care better than the private sector. I think looking just north of us

[Canada] to a government-run system, most Americans
are going to say they don't want rationing, they don't want
a bureaucracy, they don't want a big tax increase.

As the 1994 congressional election drew nearer, Gingrich and
his team expanded that argument beyond health care to disparage
Clinton's entire governing philosophy.

In a CNN appearance on August 8, Gingrich said:

The Clintons [believe] that the American people are too
dumb to provide for their own health care. The Clintons
believe that government is smarter and if only you had a
bureaucrat watching over you, you'd lead a better life. And
so they—I think this is a sincere belief—they honestly
believe that they, through government, by raising your
taxes and taking away your money, can make better
decisions for you than you can on your own.

Republicans were able to execute this strategy after stoking fear
about a plan that wasn't even put into place yet, whereas in 2005,
Democrats let fear of the "big government" tag stop them from holding up a concrete success to make the case for effective liberal government.

TAKING ON INEFFECTIVE GOVERNMENT

While liberals should highlight areas where our government has
been effective, we need not be knee-jerk about it. If we are blind to
ineffective programs, we will undercut our message about responsible government and the "big government" stereotypes will persist.

Attacking ineffectiveness shows we understand the difference between good and bad government.

Under George W. Bush's administration there has been ample opportunity to criticize ineffective government. Take education, where educators and school administrators are chafing under the misguided federal mandates of No Child Left Behind; or toxic waste cleanup, where taxpayers are paying more, polluters are paying less, and the pace of cleanup has dramatically slowed; or welfare, as poverty has risen on the Republicans' watch. And the quintessential example of ineffective government was the pathetic response to Hurricane Katrina.

Unfortunately, during Katrina's aftermath, Democratic leaders refused to go on the offensive to explain how representative, responsive, responsible government could have made a difference in lives and property. The main Democratic criticism was "incompetence" on the part of the Bush Administration. But that told just half the story. This wasn't merely about inexperienced officials. This was about the dangerous philosophy of downsizing and dismantling government held by the Republican Party. Any party can fire a few bureaucrats when the pressure's on. Only an election can fire a party and change the ideological direction of our government. Once again, fear of being accused of supporting "big government" kept Democrats from telling the full story.

It is essential for us to make the case that without a representative, responsive, and responsible governing body, there are some things we just can't do, like effectively educate our kids and care for our elders, preserve our environment so we can live healthy and enjoyable lives, and protect our towns and cities from the horrors of natural disasters. If conservative forces succeed in continuing to erode our trust in what we can accomplish together through government, our expectations and standards will wither, our government will disintegrate from lack of support, and too many of us will fall through society's cracks.

STAY AND FIGHT

Promote the Three R's of Liberal Government

✓Don't refer to "the government" and feed the image of a distant, oppressive entity. Always speak of "our government," to accurately paint government as an extension of the people that we control and direct.

✓ Don't accept that the core debate between Democrats and Republicans is whether government should be big or small. Define liberal government as representative, responsive, and responsible, and conservative government as elitist, callous, and reckless.

✓In conversations about politics, cite examples from your community where our government makes a positive difference in people's lives, such as when veterans receive good medical care from a Veterans Administration facility or children get access to the Internet at school or in a library thanks to federal funding. At the same time, point out instances where the lack of government involvement made a situation worse, such as when electricity deregulation increased rates and degraded service.

✓Don't leave it to antigovernment conservatives to criticize our government in places where it is not working well. The more we lead the charge for reforming ineffective government, the more credibility we will have when proposing effective government solutions and the harder it will be for conservatives to exploit those examples and fan overall distrust of government.

CHAPTER 3

BUY YOUR SHARE IN AMERICA

"A strong and sound Federal tax system is essential to America's future. Without such a system, we cannot maintain our defenses and give leadership to the free world. Without such a system, we cannot render the public services necessary for enriching the lives of our people and furthering the growth of our economy."

—President John F. Kennedy, April 20, 1961

There is one day of the year when everybody consciously comes in contact with our government: Tax Day. Unfortunately, for most of us it's a bad experience. If you have to pay more than you were expecting, it feels unfair and you get angry. The process of filing is tedious. It takes an average of 28 ½ hours to fill out the forms. The instruction manual is poorly written and hard to follow. Even if you file through a professional tax preparer, it's cumbersome to organize your records. And the system is so complicated that you run the risk of missing out on deductions you're entitled to, whether you do your own taxes or not. The whole experience doesn't inspire much confidence in our government, and it doesn't leave us with a warm feeling about handing over our hard-earned money.

Yet we have chosen to govern ourselves and not be ruled by a dictator or a monarch. To have that power, we need to fund our government. Think of it as buying shares of stock in America, and with it the authority to shape our nation's policies. That was the whole point of the American Revolution—not to have cheap tea, but so that with taxation we gained representation, with the power of government resting in *our* hands.

Nevertheless, Republicans have been quite successful at promoting their antigovernment stance by denigrating taxes as inherently bad. Conservative activist Grover Norquist is the most open in talking about this "Starve the Beast" strategy. National Public Radio's Mara Liasson, in a May 2001 profile of Norquist, reported that "when the [Bush] tax cut is enacted, Grover Norquist says, there will be much less money available to the government, fewer resources that the state can use." Norquist then told Liasson, "I don't want to abolish government. I simply want to reduce it to the size where I can drag it into the bathroom and drown it in the bathtub."

Taxation has always been an issue that could burn a politician if not approached carefully. In the 16th century, Machiavelli's *The Prince* warned political leaders against "unduly weigh[ing] down [their] people" with taxes, which would "soon make [a prince] odious to his subjects."

Of course, that was a time when a prince was able to finance his government, as Machiavelli noted, by "spend[ing] that which is his own," or by "pillage, sack, and extortion, handling that which belongs to" people from foreign lands. Granted, certain conservatives are partial to overseas pillaging, but a true democracy is funded by its own people.

Therefore, despite the political difficulties, we must face up to the tax task.

As a long-term concern, if cutting taxes continues to be the only acceptable position for a politician, then Democrats will never be able to promote policies that provide publicly desired services while balancing the budget—policies based on the principle of representative, responsive, and responsible government.

As a short-term concern, the next Democrat to become president—whomever it is, and whenever it happens—will have to raise taxes. Republicans have done to our budget what William Hung did to "She Bangs." They butchered it, and we're going to have to clean up the mess.

REJECT
THE REPUBLICAN FRAME

How do Republicans dictate the terms of the tax debate? They frame it as a simple choice between cutting taxes and raising taxes. That puts Democrats in a seemingly lose-lose position. Either they take the raising taxes position, which gives Republicans the easier target, or they can embrace tax cuts and compromise the party's long-term goals for the hope of short-term gain.

The Democratic Party hasn't tried the former since Walter Mondale's presidential candidacy in 1984. With deficits exploding under President Ronald Reagan, Mondale dared to say at his nomination acceptance speech:

> *Whoever is inaugurated in January, the American people will have to pay Mr. Reagan's bills. The budget will be squeezed. Taxes will go up. And anyone who says they won't is not telling the truth to the American people . . . it must be done. Mr. Reagan will raise taxes, and so will I. He won't tell you. I just did.*

Mondale rightly understood that there was no point in winning without a mandate from the people to do what was necessary. But he was the wrong person to deliver such a message.

Mondale's plain-spoken candor actually had some short-term political benefits. He cut Reagan's lead by 6 points in the Harris poll and briefly took the lead in a *Newsweek* poll. The Reagan team, totally caught off guard, couldn't get its story straight whether it was promising no tax hikes in a second term no matter what, or leaving the door open a crack for a change in course.

However, since Mondale was vice president to Jimmy Carter—the guy Reagan beat because people felt Carter ran an ineffective government that weakened the economy—Reagan was able to regain his footing. He simply associated Mondale's proposals with the high inflation and high interest rates that persisted under the Carter-Mondale administration. He undermined Mondale's promises to cut the deficit by stressing that he had inherited deficits from Mondale and his old boss. In the end, Mondale lost his moral authority on the issue.

In 1988, presidential candidate Michael Dukakis tried to defy the Republican frame by not supporting either tax raises or tax cuts while backing a crackdown on tax cheats. But the frame held. When pressed, Dukakis wouldn't rule out tax increases, and he was portrayed as a tax raiser anyway.

In 1992, Bill Clinton didn't defy the frame. He just turned it around, having been served up a huge opening on a silver platter—after President George H. W. Bush broke his "Read My Lips. No New Taxes" pledge. Clinton campaigned on a "middle-class tax cut" and attacked Bush as a tax raiser. Bush, sans moral authority, had no escape.

Clinton won, but the Republican frame was still in place: tax cuts always good, tax increases always bad. So in 1993, when Clinton forced Democrats to bite the bullet in the name of deficit reduction, shelve plans for a middle-class tax cut, and pass a tax increase mainly on the wealthy, he was working without a mandate, and he paid a heavy price. He couldn't secure any bipartisan support, and the deficit reduction package passed by a single vote in both the House and Senate. The policy shift on taxes rankled the public, and those who voted for the bill were highly vulnerable, contributing to the loss of Congress to the Republicans the following year. Those defeated included the freshman congresswoman Marjorie Margolies-Mezvinsky, who cast the deciding vote.

TAX HIKES KILL JOBS! DESTROY ECONOMIES! RUIN OUR—ER, SCRATCH THAT

Then a funny thing happened: Clinton's deficit reduction plan worked. In 1996 the deficit had been cut by 60 percent and the economy improved, creating 10 million jobs. Republicans who had been preaching that Clinton's tax policy would bring about economic apocalypse looked foolish.

That's the kind of sea-changing development that can be used to reframe a debate.

Instead of continuing to accept the Republican frame, Clinton could have articulated that Democrats support levels of taxation that are *fair* to people at all income levels and *adequate* enough to carry out the responsibilities that the people ask of their government. Republicans, on the other hand, support *inadequate* taxation, so our government can't properly function, with *unfair* tax giveaways to their corporate donors and those who make more than $200,000 each year.

That's a frame consistent with the principle of representative, responsive, and responsible government. It does not say that tax cuts are always good, or that tax increases are always good. It simply makes the commonsense point that a responsible level of taxation, properly financing our government, is healthy for our overall quality of life.

However, Clinton did not seize the opportunity. He stuck with the Republican frame and continued to argue that tax cuts are the path to economic growth.

At an October 1995 fundraiser, Clinton told the crowd, "I think I raised [taxes] too much." He then campaigned for re-election on another promise of tax cuts, though he distinguished his plan from his opponent's by promising fiscally prudent "targeted tax cuts," as opposed to a "risky $550 billion tax scheme" which would lead to cuts in Medicare and Social Security. It became a debate over whose tax cuts were better, and with a good economy at his back, Clinton won.

The same debate repeated itself in 2000. Then–Texas governor George W. Bush honed the argument against targeted tax cuts by accusing Al Gore of being a "pick and chooser," while Bush would cut taxes for "everybody who pays taxes." This was no knockout punch— again, Bush's arguments did not win him the most votes—but it did find the rhetorical weakness in the case for "targeted tax cuts." If tax cuts were so wonderful, why shouldn't everybody get them?

And so, after three elections in a row where one professed tax cutter faced off against another, President Bush was unabashed at claiming a mandate for huge cuts. Democrats, having accepted the benefit of tax cuts, had no principled foundation with which to fight back. Bush quickly rammed a tax cut bill through Congress with bipartisan support.

Even though Clinton put the nation on sound fiscal footing, he left his handiwork extremely vulnerable by not articulating the guiding principles that got the job done. Bush took full advantage and put Clinton's balanced budget in the shredder.

Still, no presidential candidate in modern memory, Republican or Democratic, has won without promising tax cuts. Might it just be the case that the public will never swallow assurances of "fair and adequate" taxation if it means tax raises for some in the short term? Is it possible that the best Democrats can ever hope to do is merely slow down the GOP drive to slash taxes and gut government?

Absolutely not.

FOUR OUT OF FIVE AMERICANS AGREE: TAXES A-OKAY FOR THE USA!

In the previous chapter I cited a survey conducted by Stan and Anna Greenberg that indicated it's not taxes themselves that upset Americans, but how the money is used. Yet public understanding of the importance of taxes runs deeper than that. The Greenbergs also asked whether respondents didn't "mind paying taxes" for various reasons. Here are some of the results, with percentages combining those who "strongly" and "somewhat" agreed with the following statements:

- I don't mind paying taxes because my taxes contribute to making sure we have public schools, clean streets, public safety and a national defense, and a cleaner environment: 84 percent (61 percent strongly)
- I don't mind paying takes because my taxes are part of my contribution to society as a citizen of the United States: 81 percent (56 percent strongly)

REPUBLICAN PORK PRODUCTS

The rap on liberals is that we want to raise taxes through the roof and spend your hard-earned money on every pork project that comes down the pike. Not fair! There are all sorts of Republican "programs" any self-respecting liberal would never waste a taxpayer dollar on. (Can you guess which of the following is for real?)

Reverse Embed Program

It's one thing to pay Army public relations staff to escort reporters riding around with our military in Iraq, but it's just exorbitant to spend money on embedding generals and colonels inside our nation's newsrooms. Besides, feeding propaganda to right-wing bloggers is much simpler and cheaper.

United States Institute for Peace*

There's no point spending $16 million a year on this institution after George W. Bush named to its board a guy who attacked politicians (including Bush) who called Islam a "religion of

- I don't mind paying taxes because I want government to play a strong role in helping people, when in need: 76 percent (46 percent strongly)
- I don't mind paying taxes because it is my contribution to make sure our government helps create opportunities and keeps the economy growing: 75 percent (43 percent strongly)

peace" and lamented that "what war had achieved for Israel, diplomacy has undone."

Congressional Junket Fund

We do want to end the practice of corporate lobbyists paying for trips taken by Senators and Representatives, but golf outings, steak dinners, and kept mistresses do not belong on the taxpayer tab.

Bill Bennett Anti-Crime Ad Campaign

Marketing free vasectomies and fallopian tube ties to African-Americans is not an appropriate use of McGruff the Crime Dog.

Nuclear and Chemical Plant Security

The shoring up of sensitive national assets is long overdue, but liberals wouldn't contract out the business to Dubai-Taliban Security Systems Inc.

U.S. Institute for Peace is for real.

As you can see, people not only recognize a link between paying taxes and loving their country, but they also grasp the connection between paying taxes and attaining desired services and societal goals.

And it's not just that one poll. The *Los Angeles Times* has asked the public twice in recent years, "which do you think is more effective in stimulating the nation's economy," tax cuts or improvements to the country's infrastructure. Infrastructure spending wins by a mile: 60 percent to 34 percent in the January '05 poll. The *Times* polls also identified a statistical tie between our desire for tax cuts versus paying down the national debt. But an Associated Press poll taken just before the 2004 election asked, "If you had to choose, would you prefer balancing the budget or cutting taxes?" Balancing the budget prevailed by a wide margin: 66 percent to 31 percent.

If the public is not hopelessly infatuated with tax cuts, then why are Democrats so reluctant to make the case for fair and adequate taxation?

Because the above data only prove that people understand the connection between taxes and representative, responsive, and responsible government. It is not contradictory for people to also understand that paying taxes does not automatically guarantee high-quality government. Before a "fair and adequate taxation" platform can win, people must be convinced that their political leaders can be trusted to spend their money according to their wishes.

Recent history helps make the argument. Clinton's fair and adequate taxation led to a balanced budget, a growing economy, low interest rates, and reduced poverty. Bush Jr.'s unfair taxation led to inadequate resources. Middle-class families are having a harder time sending their kids to college because public college tuitions have gone up while federal Pell Grants have been cut. Poverty has risen while funding for job training is slashed. Veterans can't afford decent health care because Veterans Administration spending can't keep pace with health costs. Our nation's leadership role in scientific and medical innovations is declining, while a clampdown on federal investment is prompting companies to move research jobs to overseas labs. And our economy is bogged down by massive debt.

LESS PAIN, MORE GAIN

Showing how budget items affect our daily lives is not a ground-breaking concept, but it's rarely executed well. People know that numbers can be sliced and diced beyond recognition. A headline like "Ten Percent Cut in [Federal Program With Big Acronym]" often won't resonate because it's not necessarily the case that less funding equals less service and lower quality of life.

However, people know what's going on in their families and their communities. Many people feel the squeeze on college and health care costs, experience the fact that good-paying jobs are disappearing, and understand that wages are stagnating. We need to connect on that real-world level first and then show how unfair taxation deprives our government of the resources necessary to address these problems. That means we need to lead with the bottom line—"we're struggling with sending our kids to college"—and not with the wonky details—"tax cuts forced tuition increases and Pell Grant cuts."

Speaking of pain, let's be careful not to sell fair and adequate taxation with an "eat your spinach" style of message. In the 1992 Democratic presidential primary, former Sen. Paul Tsongas earned some niche appeal by refusing to embrace a middle-class tax cut, saying harshly, "I'm not Santa Claus." But Clinton was able to pierce his bubble by retorting, "I am tired of what is cold-blooded being passed off as courageous," and "People have been plundered for a decade. It's time to ease up." Clinton preached fairness for a brighter tomorrow, while Tsongas preached pain, and the uplifting vision won.

Politicians shouldn't be scolding people that they have to suck it up and pay their taxes. You don't tell the shareholders what to do. We are the ones who decide what our government should do and how much we should pay for it. The politician's job is to help voters make informed decisions, not to condescend and shove policies down their throats. If Democrats regularly present to voters the straight dope on how we have prospered with fair and adequate taxation and how we have struggled under reckless tax cutting, while stressing that the ultimate decision on taxes rests in the people's hands, Republicans will have a tougher time charging Democrats with forcing pain on the public.

Beyond recasting the rhetoric, a substantive way Democrats could offer voters less pain without pandering is to get behind a plan to simplify the tax code and the filing process. Tax simplification has largely been pushed by conservatives. They have embraced it to sugarcoat their dream of scrapping our long-standing progressive tax system, where those with more income pay higher rates than those with less, in favor of a "flat tax," a single rate for all taxpayers. Unfortunately for conservatives, tax simplification is not sugary enough to make Americans swallow such a ludicrous idea. Voters have always recognized that the flat tax is a transparent scheme by a few wealthy Americans who'd rather shirk their patriotic obligations to their country than contribute their fair share. It is the epitome of unfair, inadequate taxation.

But there's no reason why liberals can't get behind a progressive version of tax simplification. *Simple* and *fair* are not mutually exclusive. We can strip out special-interest loopholes, straighten out unnecessary complexity, streamline the paperwork, yet still contribute sufficient revenue at rates that each of us can afford.

Whittling down our 60,000 pages of tax code is no small project, and there would be plenty of pitfalls along the way—many lines of code were inserted to appease one constituency or another. But the political and substantive benefits could be huge. If the tax code were less convoluted, it would be harder for wealthy taxpayers to exploit loopholes and duck responsibility. If it were easier for us to understand how we are paying for government, it would strengthen democracy by helping us make informed decisions about what we want our government to do. And if Democrats took the lead in making the tax filing process less painful, we'd have better Tax Day experiences, and we'd gain confidence in the ability of Democrats to manage our government and our resources.

Overall, for the liberal vision on taxes to prevail, our political leaders must show that they trust the people's ability to make informed choices, make it easier for people to choose, and honestly describe what the choices are—painting a picture of what America would be like if the people chose fair and adequate taxation, and what it will be like if unfair, inadequate taxation continues. Once they do, it will be far easier for us to encourage our fellow shareholders to meet our responsibilities and make the choices that will help America prosper.

STAY AND FIGHT

Buy Your Share in America

✓During tax time, remind yourself and others that you can't love your country and stiff it at the same time. What you *can* do is demand that the money be put to good, sensible use.

✓Be vocal about drawing connections between what happens in your community and what goes on in Washington. For example, if local taxes need to be raised to maintain services, use local media to remind your neighbors that federal tax cuts for the wealthy often leave communities without enough resources to properly educate our kids, heal our veterans, care for our elderly, police our streets, and maintain our roads.

✓Contrast the liberal vision with the conservative record: instead of supporting an irresponsible tax cut mainly for elites that has wrecked the national budget and contributed to a sluggish economy, we can restore fairness with a responsible tax raise mainly on the wealthy that will help balance the budget, improve services, lower interest rates, and grow the economy.

✓ Push Democrats to rally around a plan for tax simplification, which will redefine the party's reputation as the party that empowers the taxpayer.

CHAPTER 4

REJECT REPUBLICAN DEMOCRACY HYPOCRISY

"Foreign policy is too important to be left to specialized elites and interests. . . . All Americans must be more engaged in their nation's conduct in the world."

—Former senator Gary Hart

Not only do I want to stay and fight for America, to be honest I've never been much for traveling abroad. Instead of spending thousands of dollars to feel like an idiot asking for directions, my idea of a vacation is driving miles and miles to find the best burger (South Frio Saloon in San Antonio), steak (Doe's Eat Place in Greenville, Mississippi), chicken-fried steak (Threadgill's in Austin), or barbeque (Holy Smokes in Hatfield, Massachussets, believe it or not).

Yet it still disturbs me when a friend returns from a trip overseas talking about the deep anti-American sentiment he or she felt. Granted, such complaints can seem silly—as if you hate the Iraq

War because it spoiled your Tuscan wine country experience—but when America is perceived around the world as the bad guy, it affects us, even those of us who rarely if ever set foot in another country. When I hear those stories, it's another reminder of how conservatives have damaged our international alliances, harmed our ability to spread liberty and prosperity, and weakened our overall national security.

It has always been difficult for liberals to make the connection between how we are perceived abroad and how safe we are at home. Putting too much emphasis on how badly we want other countries to like us can come across as unprincipled, desperate, and weak. We need to better explain what we want to accomplish abroad, and how those accomplishments will pay off for America.

If we are unable to articulate how liberals would best lead the world and protect our national security, and shake the "soft" stereotype without compromising our principles, Democrats will struggle with winning elections when the nation's security is threatened.

But stereotypes die hard.

WHY KERRY LOST

The main reason John Kerry lost his bid for the presidency in 2004 is that not enough Americans trusted him with our national security. Paul Freedman, political science professor at the University of Virginia, reviewed the exit poll data for the online magazine Slate and found that nearly half of voters trusted only George W. Bush to fight terrorism, compared to about one-third who trusted only Kerry. And opinions about who was best on terrorism strongly influenced votes. Of those who trusted only Bush on terrorism, almost all voted for Bush. Same with Kerry.

Terrorism wasn't a factor in 2000, when Bush lost the popular vote, but 4 years later it worked to his advantage. For all the talk that "moral values" and religious conservatives tipped the scales in 2004, the truth is that the exit poll data on those factors is pretty much the same for 2000 and 2004. In all likelihood, whomever the Democrats put up in 2004 would have run into the same national security buzzsaw that Kerry did.

The Republican campaign against Kerry was one long string of lies, distortions, and smears designed to portray him as soft and disloyal. For example, it was often repeated by Bush and Cheney that Kerry said he would merely "wait for the next attack" before responding militarily to terrorists, meaning that he had a "September the 10th mindset." These charges were in direct response to Kerry's nomination acceptance speech, in which Kerry actually said that we needed to "get the terrorists before they get us." On several other occasions he promised to "hunt down and kill the terrorists." Another charge was that Kerry would give "France" veto power over our national security, even though Kerry had consistently pledged: "I'll never give a veto over American security to any other entity— not a nation, not a country, not an institution."

Lies, smears, and distortions are nothing new in politics. Campaigns often devolve into little more than "he said, he said." Voters, poorly informed by a vapid media, have difficulty weighing the charges and countercharges on their merits, and those that more readily fit into voters' preconceived notions are the ones that tend to stick.

In short, once you get saddled with a negative stereotype, it's a serious problem.

If your party is stereotyped as soft on national security, it doesn't matter how tough your rhetoric is. Anyone can say they're tough. Anyone can put out a policy paper that says they wouldn't be overly hesitant to use military force. The only way you can thoroughly debunk a stereotype is through high-profile action, such as winning a war like Franklin Roosevelt did with World War II, or successfully averting war without weakening America like John Kennedy did during the Cuban Missile Crisis.

Problem is, there aren't many high-profile actions that a Democrat can take to prove his or her national security mettle that don't involve occupying the Oval Office. The catch-22, of course, is that if the stereotype persists, it will be difficult for Democrats to get into the Oval Office to prove themselves.

REGAINING CREDIBILITY

One way the dynamics could change is if a presidential election were to turn on something other than national security, but that isn't something Democrats can control, no matter how often they say, "It's the economy, stupid." The voters in the end decide what issues matter most, and their priorities are influenced by national and global events. If terrorism fears subside temporarily and domestic issues move to the front burner, Democrats will have a better shot at winning a national election. And once in office, a Democratic president would have the opportunity to debunk the "soft" national security stereotype.

Another way the dynamics could change is if the public comes to perceive a Republican president as a failure on national security. That's what happened to George H. W. Bush in 1992 with regard to the economy. After a long stretch during which Republicans were considered superior to Democrats on economic issues, Bush presided over a recession while breaking his biggest campaign promise on taxes. Suddenly, Republican claims to economic superiority became empty, and voters were willing to give a Democrat a fresh look.

In 2004, George W. Bush ran the risk of being perceived as a national security failure. A majority of voters, 52 percent, said the Iraq War was going "badly." But that negative assessment was countered by the solid approval Bush had for handling terrorism. In turn, just enough voters who thought Iraq was going badly cast their ballots for Bush anyway, allowing him to get to 51 percent of the popular vote. This is an indicator of how bad things would have to get for the public to definitively conclude that a Republican president has lost credibility on national security and in turn be willing to give a Democrat a chance to show that he or she could do better.

But since we can't control global events, does that mean it's not worth our time, and not worth the political risk, to talk global policy? No. It won't matter if Republicans lose credibility if Democrats aren't taken seriously. And if we only discuss foreign policy intermittently, at politically opportunistic times, we won't be taken seriously. We need to fully flesh out a long-term, comprehensive national security strategy and show how liberals will make America safe and secure.

A LIBERAL FOREIGN POLICY VISION

Someone has already made great strides in articulating a liberal foreign policy vision. His name is George W. Bush.

In his 2005 inaugural address, Bush said:

[A]s long as whole regions of the world simmer in resentment and tyranny—prone to ideologies that feed

hatred and excuse murder—violence will gather, and multiply in destructive power, and cross the most defended borders, and raise a mortal threat.

There is only one force of history that can break the reign of hatred and resentment, and expose the pretensions of tyrants, and reward the hopes of the decent and tolerant, and that is the force of human freedom.

We are led, by events and common sense, to one conclusion: The survival of liberty in our land increasingly depends on the success of liberty in other lands. The best hope for peace in our world is the expansion of freedom in all the world.

And, 14 months prior, Bush said:

Sixty years of Western nations excusing and accommodating the lack of freedom in the Middle East did nothing to make us safe—because in the long run, stability cannot be purchased at the expense of liberty.

As long as the Middle East remains a place where freedom does not flourish, it will remain a place of stagnation, resentment, and violence ready for export. And with the spread of weapons that can bring catastrophic harm to our country and to our friends, it would be reckless to accept the status quo.

This lofty talk about democracy rubs liberals the wrong way because Bush has used it to retroactively justify an unnecessary, counterproductive war in Iraq, and he or some future conservative president may use it to justify future unnecessary, counterproductive wars. What is often missed, though, is that Bush is justifying a conservative foreign policy using liberal arguments. He is not saying that the "one force" that can end the threat of terrorism is brute military force, but "the force of human freedom." He is arguing that America has to play a proactive, positive role in the world to deny terrorist leaders the popular support they need to replenish and grow their ranks.

This is a view that would have been mocked as hippie foolishness if stated on September 12, 2001. And it is a view that Democrats would never have been able to pull off on their own because it plays into the stereotype of weakness and unwillingness to use military force when necessary. But Bush's attempt to swipe liberal rhetoric and affix it to a conservative policy provides a fresh opening for liberals. He has given us the ability to make the pragmatic case that a foreign policy strategy primarily based on human rights for all is far better for our national security than one primarily based on the unilateral display of military power.

We don't want to fall into the trap of taking the opposite stance of every single thing that comes out of Bush's mouth. If we did that in this case, we would be taking the view that we don't care whether people in other countries live under oppression. That is a cold, self-ish vision that does not square with liberal values. At the same time, we don't want to fall into the trap of accepting that the only way to spread democracy and freedom is the Bush way. More importantly, we cannot accept that Bush and the Republican Party mean what they say when talking of democracy.

In painting a liberal foreign policy vision, what we should do is: 1) Highlight where Bush is actively *preventing the spread of freedom*, 2) use those examples to explain the true nature of conservative foreign policy goals, and how they undermine our national security, and 3) compare that with a liberal foreign policy, based on *promoting credible democracy* and *eradicating poverty*, which would defeat the terrorist threat and provide long-term global stability.

DEMOCRACY HYPOCRISY

Few Democratic members of Congress and few members of the Washington punditocracy question Bush's sincerity when it comes to advancing freedom and liberty. They should.

People who hear the current rhetoric on Iraq might assume that the Arab and Muslim worlds are making progress on democratic reforms, however slowly, thanks to Bush. But there are plenty of places where Bush is directly harming the cause of freedom. To expose them is to call into question the stated foreign policy goals of conservatives. That opens the door to explaining what conservatives' *actual* foreign policy goals are.

Look at Pakistan. Its leader, Pervez Musharraf, is a military strongman who took power in a 1999 coup. Bush strengthened ties with him following September 11 and has sat idly by while Musharraf has broken promises to restore democracy. Musharraf has rewritten his country's constitution to give himself more powers, and he has jailed political opponents, tortured journalists, and even used his military to murder farmers who laid claim to the land they work. Yet Bush responded in 2005 by ending a 15-year ban on selling Pakistan F-16 fighter jets. (Bush had previously lifted an overall ban on aid that President Clinton imposed after Musharraf's coup.)

Or take the Sudan. Bush has said that he wouldn't let another genocide occur "on my watch." But after the Sudanese government began its campaign of genocide in 2003, Bush continued his efforts to renew ties with the country's brutal leaders that Bill Clinton had cut. In April 2005, a top Bush State Department official lowballed the death toll while being led on a tour of Sudan by its vice president. And in February 2006 another State spokesperson further downplayed the situation, saying that while "genocide has occurred" previously, "there isn't large-scale organized violence taking place today," just "incidents" and "small attacks." That prompted United Press International's David Lepeska to report, in understated fashion, "the scene on the ground belies the American assertions." All of these moves sent signals to the Sudanese government that it can keep committing atrocities without fear of repercussion.

Or consider, when Bush desperately tried to salvage a deal that would have outsourced the operations of six U.S. ports to the United Arab Emirates. Part of his argument was that we needed to "strengthen our friendships and relationships with moderate Arab countries." But since when did "moderate" apply to a country that is ruled by royals and that literally doesn't hold elections for any government offices? Furthermore, about 80 percent of the oil-rich nation's population are migrant workers with no rights. Human Rights Watch reports that there are "persistent credible reports of abuses committed by employers" in the UAE, such as unpaid wages, "unsafe working environments," and "squalid...labor camps."

The list goes on. The notorious dictatorship Equatorial Guinea, dubbed the "oil star" of Africa's Gulf of Guinea, is enjoying closer ties to America since Bush took office. Secretary of State Condoleezza Rice even publicly pronounced the country's tyrannical leader a "good friend." Egypt holds an election in which the current dictator decides who can run, and it's blessed by the White House. In Jordan, press freedoms and political dissent are curtailed without the nation jeopardizing its free trade pact with the United States. In our own hemisphere, Bush helped engineer a coup of the democratically elected leader in Haiti and tacitly supported a failed coup of the democratically elected leader of Venezuela.

Perhaps most telling is the State Department's Middle East Partnership Initiative. It's billed as the "primary" tool to support the "strategy of freedom in the Middle East." But the Boston Globe found that the vast majority of its funds have gone to propping up dictators.

Freedom is not on the march. It is in retreat.

In the past, when liberals have called out such devil's bargains as violations of American ideals, conservatives would call us dangerously naïve and argue that supporting friendly dictators is just what you have to do to protect American interests. But now we have Bush's own words on our side: "Sixty years of Western nations excusing and accommodating the lack of freedom in the Middle East did nothing to make us safe—because in the long run, stability cannot be purchased at the expense of liberty."

The argument is not that Bush shouldn't be promoting democracy. The argument is that Bush and his fellow conservatives are totally insincere about promoting democracy. Their game is the same ol' shortsighted, reckless unilateralism—aggressively exerting dominance over far-flung regions of the world, particularly those regions with strategically important natural resources. Never mind if such a strategy leaves, to quote Bush again, "whole regions of the world [to] simmer in resentment and tyranny—prone to ideologies that feed hatred and excuse murder."

PROMOTE CREDIBLE DEMOCRACY

It's not enough to make clear that advancing democracy isn't actually a foreign policy goal of conservatives. And it's not enough for liberals to simply say "democracy," "freedom," and "liberty" a lot and call that a policy. Liberals need to show that they not only have superior strategic goals compared with conservatives, but also that they know how to pragmatically achieve those goals.

A liberal foreign policy would put America squarely behind promoting "credible democracy" throughout the world. By "credible" I mean democracy that is mainly homegrown and indisputably the will of a sovereign people. When a new form of government is imposed from the outside at the point of a gun, and the country holding the gun plays a direct role in staffing the new government, then the legitimacy of the new government will be dubious. And that creates the conditions for lingering resentment and ongoing violence.

How can America promote something that must be homegrown? How can we help the people of the world take control of their own governments while also maintaining global security and stability? Here are four key steps (partially inspired by the Center for American Progress's national security strategy, "Integrated Power"):

1. WORK WITH INTERNATIONAL INSTITUTIONS AND COALITIONS.

No one country, not even a superpower, can successfully apply diplomatic and economic pressure on a dictatorship. For example, if one country cuts off trade with a dictatorship but other countries step up trade, the sanction has no impact. But if large coalitions of nations, or international institutions such as the United Nations or NATO, apply such pressure over a sustained period of time, then a dictator is more likely to see the writing on the wall and eventually cede his grip on power.

Working with others when using "carrots and sticks" also adds legitimacy. It signals that America is not acting in narrow self-interest (e.g., control of natural resources), which would not attract the support of a broad coalition, but that it is acting with clear moral purpose (e.g., freedom and human rights for all peoples).

2. DON'T PLAY FAVORITES.

When America deals with another country, instead of only talking to the people in power or to a single opposition party, we should deal with groups representing *all* peoples and parties representing *all* ideologies in that country. That way it will be evident that America is not trying to dictate who is in power in other countries for its own ends, but that we are willing to work with whomever sovereign peoples choose to represent them, now or in the future.

3. LEAD BY EXAMPLE.

America cannot successfully promote human rights abroad if it does not practice what it preaches. If we are going to insist that other nations respect international laws, then we must do so as well. If we ratify the UN Convention on Torture, as we have, then we should abide by it and not try to weasel out of it. We should not be afraid of international human rights standards. We should proudly set high standards for the world to follow.

4. STOP NUCLEAR PROLIFERATION.

The closer an autocratic nation comes to obtaining nuclear weapons, the harder it becomes to exert diplomatic and economic pressure and push it toward democratization. Most notably, North Korea has been able to obtain at least two nuclear bombs during George W. Bush's time in office, greatly increasing its bargaining power. That's left America with only unpleasant options: offer concessions in exchange for getting rid of nuclear weapons, or do nothing and risk those weapons being sold to terrorists in the hope that the dictatorship will eventually collapse.

Attacking countries on false claims of their possessing nuclear arms, as Bush did in Iraq, damages America's credibility. The building of permanent military bases in Iraq isn't helping. It sends a message that "regime change" of other nearby countries we don't like, such as Iran, is on tap, giving a huge incentive for those in the cross-hairs to develop nuclear weapons as a defensive measure. Nor is developing new nuclear weapons, as Bush is also doing, a winning strategy because it undermines our ability to pressure and persuade other countries from pursuing such weapons for themselves. The *best* strategy for us is to junk our current unilateralist foreign policy and lead an international effort against nuclear proliferation, supporting the inspectors at the UN's International Atomic Energy Agency, strengthening and enforcing the Nuclear Non-Proliferation Treaty, and working with Russia to secure its loose nuclear material.

ERADICATE POVERTY

Liberals also recognize that democracy can't take root in places where people remain oppressed by poverty. Freedom doesn't mean a whole lot to a family without food. Since it is in America's national security interest to promote credible democracy, it is also in our interest to take up the call by economist Jeffrey Sachs of Columbia University's Earth Institute to eliminate "extreme poverty," in which people live on less than a dollar a day, by 2025. Sachs notes that such an ambitious goal has to be a global effort involving significant financial resources geared toward helping poor countries feed themselves. Sachs recommends increasing America's foreign aid budget from 0.14 percent of our gross national product to 0.70 percent (a goal also embraced by the ONE Campaign, which organized the Live8 concerts), using "clinical economics" to continually assess how effectively money is being spent and make improvements as needed, and empowering and revitalizing international institutions such as the World Bank, the International Monetary Fund, and UN agencies such as the World Health Organization and UNICEF.

Similarly, Sherle R. Schwenninger, of the World Policy Institute and New American Foundation think tanks, called for a "New International Deal" in the pages of *The Nation* magazine. Like Franklin Roosevelt's New Deal, which harnessed the power of the federal government to create jobs through public works projects, a New International Deal would use international institutions to create jobs and "build a global middle class."

Of course, big ideas cost money. But war costs more, in money and our security. Liberals need to make the case that a financial commitment to eradicating poverty is essential to spreading democracy, reducing resentment, suffocating terrorism, and preventing far more expensive military actions that cost lives as well.

WHAT ABOUT WAR?

Discussions about foreign policy often turn on the question, "Under what circumstances would you go to war?" But it's a mistake to base a Democratic foreign policy vision on the answer. A foreign policy should be based on goals. Freedom and security for all, poverty for none—those are goals. War is a tactic, not a goal.

And it is generally a bad tactic. People end up dying, and wars often cause more problems than they solve.

So what is the liberal position on war? War is justified when America or one of its allies has been attacked; when there is an imminent threat that a pre-emptive attack could prevent; or when a defenseless people are facing slaughter.

We are experiencing one of those circumstances now. Al Qaeda has declared war on the United States and attacked us (as well as the citizens of many other countries). Military force must be used to capture or kill Al Qaeda members and stop future terrorist operations.

Furthermore, while military action would be rarer under a liberal foreign policy, taking military action in times of crisis would be easier to execute. Once it is understood throughout the world that America is constantly working with other nations to ensure freedom and prosperity for all peoples, a U.S.-led military action would not spark worldwide suspicion, and in turn it would not have the same negative political ramifications as it does under a conservative foreign policy.

However, there may be situations in which, even if war is justified, there are other practical tactics to use that carry fewer risks. South Africa's oppression of blacks during Apartheid ended thanks to economic sanctions. The tyrannical Soviet Union fell not after a hasty act of war but with a patient policy of containment. If other options are available that will leave fewer people dead and provoke fewer unintended consequences, they should be used.

Does such a caveat leave liberals open to the charge that they can't be trusted to pull the trigger when it counts? Yes. Is it a fair charge? No. But as I argued earlier, the "weak" stereotype simply can't be shaken until we can obtain power and prove otherwise by our actions. There is no short-term political benefit in trashing our principles and changing our policy views in a transparent attempt to sound hawkish.

Some conservative-leaning Democrats who supported the Iraq War portray themselves as "National Security Democrats." They want liberals to stop giving war a bad name. And they like using euphemisms for war, particularly the term *power*. Senator Joe Biden praises "the transformative capability of military power." *The New Yorker*'s George Packer laments that Democrats don't "back up" talk of liberal internationalism "with power." *The New Republic*'s Peter

Beinart calls for a "post-Vietnam liberalism that embrace[s] U.S. power" to be used for "aggressive efforts to democratize the Muslim world."

This is wrong substantively and futile politically. A core liberal value is that war is generally bad, morally and pragmatically. Promoting credible democracy and eradicating poverty is ultimately what will defeat terrorism, keep America safe, and build a durable peace. We have George W. Bush's words to help make that case, and we have George W. Bush's actions to show that a conservative foreign policy harms our national security.

STAY AND FIGHT

Reject Republican Hypocrisy

✓When engaging the media, and in casual conversation, base your foreign-policy arguments on a liberal vision of promoting credible democracy and eradicating poverty using strong international alliances to achieve national and global security. At the same time, oppose the conservative policy of using our military to exert unilateral influence abroad, breeding resentment and fueling terrorism.

✓Reject the notion that conservatives have a sincere interest in supporting democracy by citing the litany of examples in which the Bush White House has stifled freedom abroad and supported dictators.

✓Foreign policy experts rarely speak in laymen's terms, cultivating a mystique, and mainstream news outlets do a poor job of putting international news in an understandable context. So it takes extra effort to educate yourself. But the world of blogs

can help. Here are a few that cover the spectrum of Democratic and liberal thinking: tomdispatch.com, democracyarse-
nal.org, armscontrolwonk.com, juancole.com, abuaardvark.
typepad.com, americanfootprints.com, thewashingtonnote.
com, justworldnews.org, and warandpiece.com.

✓The pool of foreign-policy pundits on which TV and radio
shows rely tends to lean conservative, regardless of party affiliation. When you see sharp liberal analysis from the blogosphere, or from magazines such as *The Nation, The American
Prospect,* or *Mother Jones,* contact TV and radio talk shows, call
their attention to the articles and urge that the authors be
booked as guest experts.

✓Support the efforts of the Global Marshall Plan Initiative,
calling for new investment to eradicate poverty, promote sus-
tainable development, and protect the environment. Go to
globalmarshallplan.org for more information.

CHAPTER 5

DEFUSE THE CULTURE WAR

Christians did not start the culture war but...we are going to end it.

God forbid that we who were born into the blessings of a Christian America should let our patrimony slip like sand through our fingers and leave to our children the bleached bones of a godless secular society.
—Dr. D. James Kennedy, founder of Center for Reclaiming America for Christ

[handwritten: extreme rhetoric]

Conservatives like war so much they promote one here at home: a culture war, where they portray themselves as heroic defenders of faith and family doing battle against an army of godless homosexual baby-killing hybrid-car-driving liberals. Of course, only one side believes that an elite group should dictate morality for the entire nation, and it ain't us liberals.

The assumption among many in Washington—Democrats and Republicans—is that certain hot-button lifestyle issues work against Democrats. This assumption can drive Democratic politicians to desperately seek elusive middle ground using poll-tested rhetoric, or to try to duck the issues altogether.

Let's question that assumption.

In 1992, Pat Buchanan delivered a prime-time convention speech on behalf of George H. W. Bush and said, "There is a religious war

[handwritten: I like this part of the book]

going on in our country for the soul of America. It is a cultural war, as critical to the kind of nation we will one day be as was the Cold War itself. And in that struggle for the soul of America, Clinton and Clinton are on the other side, and George Bush is on our side." But voters didn't buy the conservative bluster. They saw the 1992 election as an opportunity to fix the sluggish economy, not as a time to wage cultural or religious civil war.

Twelve years later, fringe fundamentalist leaders contended that social issues galvanized the conservative base and gave George W. Bush the margin of victory. This isn't true. A 2000 exit poll data showed that 56 percent of the electorate believed abortion should be always or mostly legal. In 2004 the number was 55 percent, a statistically insignificant difference. There was no big influx of anti-abortion voters in 2004.

Furthermore, the 2004 exit poll found that only 37 percent of the electorate opposed any legal recognition for same-sex couples, while 60 percent supported either marriage or civil unions. Such a question wasn't asked in 2000, but let's go out on a limb and assume that pro-gay support would not have been anywhere near 60 percent back in November 2000, only a few months after Vermont became the first state to legalize civil unions. A late November 2004 Gallup poll found that 63 percent of Americans supported gays serving openly in the armed forces. Prior to 2001, according to the Center for the Study of Sexual Minorities in the military, no poll had found a majority supporting uncloseted gays in the military.

So how did Bush win in 2004 if feelings about abortion remained the same and support for gay rights was on the upswing? For one, terrorism and national security issues trumped all. For another, Bush was careful in his rhetoric about social issues, often using code words such as "culture of life" and "sanctity of marriage" that resonated with his base without fully cluing in the broad middle of the electorate. He even offered some tepid support for civil unions late in the race to avoid being perceived as rigidly antigay. (Bush won the vote among those who backed civil unions by 5 points.)

The code-word strategy may be canny, but it is not one that Democrats should emulate or that liberals should accept. Code words are intended to keep a party's ideological base at bay without alienating swing voters, but they do not help foster understanding, defuse tensions, solve problems, and build the bridges necessary to establish a solid majority. Only a candid approach can do that.

However, a candid approach that is clumsily executed will backfire. Poorly chosen words can be misinterpreted by those who don't automatically share your perspective. And when passions run high, little things can be taken as slights, alienating potential supporters.

How can Democrats avoid such missteps while being candid?

First, we can build trust by consistently rooting our positions on social and cultural issues in our principle of representative, responsive, and responsible government (and, when applicable, our foreign policy and taxation principles). Second, we can foster understanding by acknowledging and respecting opposing views without ceding our principles.

Here's how it would work with some of the most polarizing issues we face today.

REPRODUCTIVE FREEDOM

It's amazing that Democrats are still struggling with how to talk about reproductive freedom and abortion rights, considering that Roe v. Wade was decided 3 decades ago and public support for the decision remains high. During the Supreme Court confirmation process for both John Roberts and Sam Alito, surveys showed 60 percent or more wanted the new justices to uphold Roe.

Yet struggle they do. Some leading Democrats have decided that the party is too closely identified with the abortion issue. Right after the 2004 election, Senator John Kerry told a group of Democratic and liberal leaders that the party needed to make clear it "didn't like abortion." Since then, Democratic Party chair Howard Dean has taken to saying things like

> *I don't know anybody who's pro-abortion. Most people in this country would like to see the abortion rate go down. That includes Democrats and Republicans. The difference between the parties is that we believe a woman makes that decision about her health care—and they believe Tom Delay makes it.*

That's from a speech to Democrat activists in Utah in July 2005. Earlier that year, Senator Hillary Clinton made waves when she told family planning providers

> *Abortion in many ways represents a sad, even tragic choice to many, many women. . . .*
>
> *There is no reason why government cannot do more to educate and inform and provide assistance so that the choice guaranteed under our constitution either does not ever have to be exercised or only in very rare circumstances.*

The Dean and Clinton approaches are not identical, and each has some worthwhile aspects to them. But they both make one very large mistake. They concede a key principle to conservatives. They say abortion is bad.

If we join Republicans in claiming that abortion is morally wrong, then why wouldn't we also want to ban it, or at least severely restrict access to it?

Instead of ceding that principle, liberals should be articulating why we do fight so hard on this issue: because we believe that it is a moral good for women to have control over their futures, including if and when to have children. We also believe that medical decisions should remain between a woman and her doctor. Complications can arise during a pregnancy, even in the last trimester. There are times when carrying out a pregnancy can be fatal or can exacerbate serious health problems such as cancer, heart disease, and diabetes. These rare situations pose wrenching choices, but they are choices that belong to a woman and her doctor alone. A representative government respects life, liberty, and the pursuit of happiness for all of its citizens by protecting the ability for individuals to make their own moral judgments. *(example of a too-simple argument)*

Certain regulations on abortion, as Roe already allows for, do not violate the principle of representative government. Mandatory parental notification for minors is fine, as long as minors have an opportunity to go before a judge and make a case as to why such notification would be unwise (as when the pregnancy is a result of incest). In the vast majority of cases, the parents will be involved, but the minor still has some control over a choice that will impact the rest of her life, long after her parents have passed on.

Dean's core message, "we believe a woman makes that decision about her health care," is a well-intentioned attempt to apply principle, but it only addresses well the issue of late-term abortions, when there is a medical issue at hand. It is a terrible way to address the larger moral questions, as it sounds cold to treat a pregnancy as simply a "decision about her health care."

And it can come across as evasive as well. *The Washington Post Magazine* reported on a Dean visit to Oklahoma when a local reporter asked him where he was "taking the party" on abortion and gay rights. Dean responded by saying, "These are not our issues; they're Republican issues. They're the ones who talk about them all the time. We believe a woman has the right to make up her own mind about what kind of health care she needs, and that ought not to be done by Tom DeLay and the boys back in Washington." The questioner didn't buy it, retorting, "So, the Democratic Party is for abortion rights, is that what you're saying?"

However, Dean's message is crucial to handling the issue that has bedeviled Democrats in recent years, the late-term "dilation and extraction" abortion procedure that antiabortion advocates inaccurately call "partial-birth abortion." Conservatives have done a good job at portraying the procedure as a grotesque way for heartless women to terminate pregnancies, as part of a strategy to chip away at Roe and malign the morality of pro-choice Democrats. For example, an ABC news poll found that 62 percent of Americans favor a ban of the procedure. Many in Congress took such data at face value and passed a ban on the procedure in 2003—which Bush famously signed surrounded by no one but men.

But that same ABC poll also showed that if the procedure "would prevent a serious threat to the woman's health," public opinion completely flips. Then, 61 percent say it should be legal. People simply don't want their government to meddle in individual medical decisions. Dean's message would work on that score.

Fringe fundamentalist leaders have a callous agenda to deny women the right to control their own lives. They do not want women to have the ability to delay or refuse motherhood. They want to restrict not only abortion but contraception as well. (The head of the Pro-Life Action League has said, "Birth control is the kissing cousin of abortion.") They don't want teenagers to have factual sex education so they can avoid unwanted pregnancies; they peddle abstinence-only education, chock full of misinformation, in an attempt to impose their version of morality on everyone.

But those leaders do not speak for every American who thinks that life begins at conception. There are reasonable opponents of

Good abortion who are not interested in denying women the right of self-determination, who would support common-sense measures to reduce unwanted pregnancies, and who are open to voting for Democrats because of other issues. In fact, more than 20 percent of those who believe that abortion should be always or mostly illegal already voted Democrat for president in 2000 and 2004. Considering that more than 30 percent of pro-choice voters voted for Bush in those same elections, there's some reason to believe that Democrats could attract additional support among voters who consider themselves pro-life.

Good Showing respect to individual opponents of abortion and searching for common ground are sensible steps to take, so long as it is done without conceding core liberal principles.

ILLEGAL IMMIGRATION

America has been experiencing a steady growth of illegal immigration in recent years. The Pew Hispanic Center estimated that nearly 12 million undocumented migrants were living in the country as of March 2006, with more than 500,000 crossing the border each year.

The debate over how to fix a clearly broken immigration system has been largely driven by a split in the Republican Party: the nativists who despise multicultural society and want a cruel crackdown, and the corporatists who despise paying workers fair wages and want immigrants for cheap labor. Both positions are examples of the Republican Party's elitist and callous principles: one turns its back on the needy, the other exploits the needy.

But we should not choose between two flawed approaches. The Democratic Party should propose its own solution based on the liberal principle of responsible government as well as the liberal foreign policy goal of eradicating poverty abroad. The 500,000 who cross the border each year without proper documentation may be breaking the law. But so are the 1,800,000 Americans who illegally import cheap prescription drugs from Canada each year because they can't afford them at home. We don't call those people criminals, since they're only doing what they need to do to stay alive. Instead, we demand that a broken system be fixed.

Our immigration system is overwhelmed by a huge number of people who can't get good jobs at home. That's what fundamentally needs fixing.

To lift Mexico up and close the economic gap between them and us requires significant investment in Mexican infrastructure, such as transportation, energy, communication and education systems. The World Bank estimates that Mexico needs $20 billion a year for 10 years to get up to speed. Center for North American Studies chief Robert Pastor, a former national security advisor to President Jimmy Carter, has proposed a North American Investment Fund, where the U.S. and Canada chip in half of what's needed and Mexico covers the rest.

In the interim, we should support guest worker programs that can lead to citizenship. But unlike the corporate Republicans pushing such plans, we should insist that they be linked to increases in the minimum wage. Otherwise, the feel-good citizenship talk only masks an agenda to maintain an underclass of low-wage workers. Now, Democrats shouldn't expect Americans to be instantaneously enthusiastic about investing their dollars into another country. As the shareholders of a representative and responsive government, we have the right to be convinced first that it would be an effective use of taxpayer dollars and benefit America over the long haul.

Fortunately, the split within the GOP gives Democrats the

opportunity to use each faction's arguments against the other, to lay the groundwork for this alternative way. Corporate Republicans rightly note that it's impractical and prohibitively expensive to forcibly ship 12 million people, in some cases breaking up families, out of the country. Nativist Republicans call out the unwillingness of corporations to pay fair wages. Once the two sides pick apart each other's overly simplistic solutions, people's minds will at least become open to the truly comprehensive liberal solution. Then the argument can be made that it would be money well spent if it improves the quality of life of our neighbors, restores fair wages at home, relieves the pressure on our borders, and permanently fixes this broken immigration system.

EQUAL MARRIAGE RIGHTS FOR GAYS

This nation is a paradox when it comes to gays. As we have seen, a clear majority of Americans support legalizing gay partnerships as well as gays serving openly in the military. However, when the issue is strictly marriage, then a clear majority do not support equal rights for gays. Only 25 percent of respondents in the 2004 election exit poll were pro–gay marriage. By March 2006, according to the Pew Poll, support had risen to 39 percent. Still, the country is "not ready" for such a step.

Of course, the country wasn't ready for civil unions when they first happened in Vermont in 2000. Gallup found that only 42 percent of Americans supported civil unions at that time (though that was up from 28 percent in 1996). Yet the bold step was taken anyway, through the democratic process in that state. Despite the hyperbolic rhetoric from opponents of equality, civil unions became

concession makes my book more credible

part of the fabric of Vermont without sullying the sanctity of hetero-sexual marriage. Without any negative consequences to confirm people's fears, the liberal position on equal partnership rights was embraced by the broad middle 4 years later.

The biggest irony: In 2003, Democrats worried that the governor who signed civil unions into law, Howard Dean, couldn't become President. In 2004, the current conservative President, George W. Bush, refused to criticize civil unions and won a second term.

That recent history is a reminder that public opinion can be moved. Committed backers, moral legitimacy, changing circumstances, and/or new evidence can turn a minority view into a majority view and alter the behavior of professional politicians.

Still, those of us pushing for liberal social change need to be careful about mitigating the intensity of the inevitable backlash. A strong, broad backlash can set our cause back years, whereas a narrow backlash can more easily be confronted and overcome.

But fears of backlash should not fool us into timidly supporting incremental change, especially when the incremental position compromises core principles. When we are compelled to mask our principles, we send a signal that our principles are nefarious and deserve to be hidden. That is when we breed mistrust.

Take Senator Hillary Clinton's handling of gay marriage and civil unions. When asked in a 2003 CBS interview if she opposed gay marriage, she said,

I am, you know, for many reasons. I think that the vast majority of Americans find that to be something they can't agree with.

But I think most Americans are fair. And if they believe that people in committed relationships want to share their lives and, not only that, have the same rights that I do in

COMPROMISE W/O COMPROMISING VALUES

my marriage, to decide who I want to inherit my property
or visit me in a hospital, I think that most Americans would
think that that's fair....

But despite opposing marriage rights, she also rejected a constitutional amendment ensuring that gays could not marry:

Yes, I think that would be a terrible step backwards. It
would be the first time we've ever amended the Constitution
to deny rights to people.

This set of views, which Clinton shares with many other congressional Democrats, literally makes no sense. Gays should not have
the right to marry, but saying so in the Constitution would deny gays
their rights? It doesn't add up. It looks like she's nominally and
superficially opposing gay marriage because she feels she has to
politically, not because she really believes it.

Conservatives are ready to pounce on such transparent pandering. Back in 2000, after Clinton said, "Marriage has got historic, religious, and moral content that goes back to the beginning of time, and
I think a marriage is as a marriage has always been: between a man
and a woman," conservative writer Jonah Goldberg wrote, "This
quote comes not from [former GOP presidential candidate] Gary
Bauer but Hillary Clinton. (Of course, Gary Bauer would mean it
when he said it.)"

Strictly backing the incremental step—in this case, civil unions—
at the expense of the principle—a truly representative government
cannot discriminate against some of its people—led to a disingenuous approach that eroded trust and failed to reduce polarization.

Does that mean we should dump on civil unions? No. They are
a major step forward. They end discrimination in partnership benefits. But to support them out of belief in equality while rejecting

equal rights for civil marriages is logically incoherent. Instead, we should stick to principle while being open to civil unions as a way to acknowledge public hesitancy for marriage rights and mitigate the backlash.

We should cite the fact that a significant majority of the country supports equal treatment for heterosexual and homosexuals, even though many Americans are nonetheless hesitant to grant civil marriage rights to gays.

We should note that such hesitancy is understandable as gay marriage lacks tradition, and that change can be discomforting.

We should stress that any changes in church policies are strictly the business of churches and not our government, but our government is not being truly representative unless it treats everyone equally.

We should accept that civil unions are a big step toward equal treatment. And now that a few states have taken that step, hesitant Americans can see for themselves whether treating gay couples fairly has any negative impact on our communities. In turn, we should express our faith that Americans will see that our communities will actually be enriched once our government fully applies our Constitution to all.

SUVS

If you don't think of SUVs as a culture war issue, consider the theme of the song "You Do Your Thing" by the hugely popular country duo Montgomery Gentry. Eddie Montgomery defiantly sings that he won't trade "my family's safety just to save a little gas," and that he'll "pray to God any place any time," apparently suggesting that liberals want him to renounce God and get into a car accident.

Somehow the idea of representative, responsive, and responsible government, which includes the responsible managing of our energy resources, has come across as self-righteously judging other individuals. That's not a place we want to be, and it's not a place we have to be.

There's no need to attack car buyers. You can't blame folks for wanting their kids to be safe. (Although SUVs *aren't* all that safe. The Insurance Institute for Highway Safety reports that they are more often involved in fatal single-vehicle accidents than passenger cars. Yet car companies market SUVs as particularly safe. The blame for this misinformation should not fall on the buyer.) The problem is the giant legal loophole that lets auto manufacturers skirt fuel efficiency requirements.

For years, the law has said a manufacturer's passenger car fleet must average 27.5 miles per gallon, but for the "light truck" fleet, only 21. Around the time that law was passed, light trucks were mainly for commercial and agriculture use and made up only one-fifth of the market. Since then, car makers have abused the law. They built SUVs that were technically light trucks and then marketed them for widespread passenger use. Now, more than half of car sales are light trucks. The gas savings we had, after the law initially passed, are fading away. What was initially a reasonable regulation has become a perverse incentive for companies to make far more gas guzzlers than our environment can afford.

It can be a reasonable regulation again if the loophole is closed. Then, noncommercial SUVs would be as fuel efficient as other passenger cars, and the choice of what kind of car to buy would be far less politically and culturally divisive. That wouldn't be the end of our energy problems by a long shot, but we'd be taking a step toward reducing our oil dependency.

But instead of closing the loophole, President Bush has solidified it. In March 2006, he announced a complicated set of new rules (to be implemented beginning with 2008 model vehicles) that create higher standards for smaller SUVs and lower ones for bigger SUVs, further creating incentives for manufacturers to flood the market with vehicles that waste our resources.

Yet increasing fuel efficiency standards—for all cars, SUV and otherwise—is widely popular. In a June 2005 survey of 1,000 people by Yale University, a whopping 89 percent of Americans believed that requiring manufacturers to make more fuel efficient cars was a "good" or "very good" idea.

Considering how many SUVs are on the road, that means that plenty of SUV buyers are actually supportive of higher standards. There's no need to alienate those folks by levying personal criticism of their priorities. Target the politicians who are not being responsive to public desires and who are irresponsibly managing our resources.

OFFENSIVE CONTENT ON TV AND RADIO

It's probably not accurate to say that there is a singular liberal position on the issue of objectionable material on the public airwaves. Liberals are traditionally known for supporting free artistic expression, believing that truly representative and responsive government does not seek to silence the views of some of its citizens. However, there are also liberals who believe that a representative and responsive government would act on behalf of those parents who feel that they can't raise their children as they see fit without some government assistance.

As for me, I'm basically in the former camp. Fears that the culture is corrupting our children have always struck me as unfounded. Every generation's parents freak out about what their kids are hearing and watching and forget that their parents did the same to them.

The infamous "Porn Rock" Senate hearings of 1985, in hindsight, perfectly capture this cycle. The Senate was responding to pressure from the Parents Music Resource Center (PMRC), founded by then–Senator Al Gore's wife, Tipper, after she bought Prince's *Purple Rain* for her daughter Karenna, unaware of its sexually explicit lyrics.

Presenters at the hearing took pains to say that what they were upset about was completely different from what past generations were upset about. The PMRC's Susan Baker testified that "the material we are concerned about cannot be compared with 'Louie Louie,' Cole Porter, Billie Holliday, et cetera."

However, Baker's testimony followed a presentation of two music videos that were cited as representative of the problem but might be considered wholesome nostalgia of a more innocent age by today's parents: Van Halen's "Hot For Teacher" and Twisted Sister's "We're Not Going To Take It." (Soon after Baker's testimony, another witness criticized "We're Not Going To Take It" as "a video in which the band members proceed to beat up daddy, who will not let them rock.")

But even though I would contend that videos like "Hot For Teacher" are not responsible for rapes, suicides, and teenage pregnancies—as the PMRC argued at the time—it is not my or anyone else's place to tell someone what material they should let their kids have access to. If parents want more help in raising their kids as they see fit, that should not raise free speech concerns, so long as our government isn't directly restricting anyone's speech. Individual parents can deny materials to their kids, and private retail outlets can choose not to stock certain items, but a government is overstepping its bounds if it starts banning or regulating expression.

The PMRC's key recommendation—voluntary warning labels on records with explicit lyrics—did not require our government to cross that constitutional line (though using a Senate hearing to push such a recommendation legitimately raised concerns among free speech advocates that government censorship could be around the corner). Furthermore, the warning-label policy has been in place for 2 decades now, and artistic expression is alive and well. A giant chain like Wal-Mart, with a policy against selling items with warning labels, may restrict distribution of some CDs. However, that's not government censorship, it does not violate the First Amendment, and it has nothing to do with the principle of representative government.

In 1995, debate over whether our government should require all new TV sets to include a "V-Chip"—giving parents the ability to block access to programs that carry certain ratings—also sparked censorship concerns. As with the earlier warning-label debate, the proposal on its own did not cross the censorship line. It was simply giving parents a tool so they could implement their own household rules. But during the course of the debate, elected officials were hinting at stiffer measures against the entertainment industry if the V-Chip didn't lead to more programming that was to their liking. Again, free speech advocates were understandably concerned about a slippery slope, and they fought the V-Chip. They lost the battle but not the war, as the V-Chip has done nothing to squelch artistic expression on TV.

Looking back at the "Porn Rock" and "V-Chip" episodes, we can actually see how the two liberal perspectives can come together under the principle of representative, responsible, and responsive government: our government should represent all Americans by respecting free speech and refusing to regulate content, while responding to parental concerns by helping provide tools for parents to enforce their own rules.

Free speechers should not dismiss concerned parents as prudish fascists, and concerned parents should not disparage free speechers

(continued on page 88)

LIBERAL ROAD TRIP!

There are cool cultural monuments to the liberal ideals of freedom and equality located all throughout America, in both red states and blue. So grab the kids (if you got 'em), pile in the car, and take back your country, one gift shop at a time.

The National Great Blacks In Wax Museum, Baltimore, MD

The notion of enshrining black leaders in wax may sound like a goof, but it's actually a great way to display all the ways in which African-Americans have furthered our nation. The slave ship and lynching exhibits are gut-wrenching.

Jimmy Carter Library and Museum, Atlanta, GA

Learn how Carter forged peace between Israel and Egypt. Hear Carter recount his term while standing in a replica of his Oval Office. See all the weird junk that other heads of state gave Carter as gifts during official visits.

National Cowgirl Museum and Hall of Fame, Fort Worth, TX

From Sacagawea to Annie Oakley to Laura Ingalls Wilder, from ranchers to bootmakers to rodeo performers, see how women shaped the American West through interactive exhibits and films.

Annual Woody Guthrie Folk Festival, Okemah, OK

Come to the birthplace of the legendary and influential political folk singer on the week of his July 14th birthday, for a long weekend of folk and country music. Also, check out the Woody Guthrie boyhood home, the Woody Guthrie water towers, and the Woody Guthrie landmark carved out of a dead cedar tree by a local "chainsaw artist."

Alabama Civil Rights Museum Trail

Covering Birmingham, Montgomery, Selma, and Tuskegee, you'll hit the Rosa Parks Museum, the Wall of Tolerance, and the Tuskegee Airmen training site.

National Chávez Center, Keene, CA

Honoring the life of farm worker organizer and advocate César Chávez, the center currently comprises a memorial garden and visitor center showing films and exhibits, but a complete museum is in the works.

Grand Staircase–Escalante National Monument, UT

If you want to explore a beautiful spot of public land under siege from oil companies, but the Arctic National Wildlife Refuge is too far out of the way, consider this 1.7 million acre span of multihued canyons and cliffs. President Clinton designated it a national monument in 1996, but corporations are pushing for at least a partial rollback.

American Labor Museum, Haledon, NJ

Located in a Victorian home that is known as the Botto House, where silk mill workers once organized a famous 20,000-person,

(continued)

LIBERAL ROAD TRIP! (CONT.)

5-month strike in 1913, the museum features artifacts and gardens that illustrate the immigrant worker experience.

Women's Rights National Historic Park, Seneca Falls, NY

Visit the chapel where the first Women's Rights Convention took place in 1848. See the home of feminist pioneer Elizabeth Cady Stanton. Then head on over to the nearby National Women's Hall of Fame.

Crawford Peace House, Crawford, TX

The home base of Cindy Sheehan's one-woman protest of the Iraq War during George W. Bush's 2005 summer vacation continues to host seminars, meetings, and workshops.

United States Vice Presidential Museum at the Dan Quayle Center, Huntington, IN

Round out your liberal road trip with a stop at this monument to the life of our nation's most mocked vice president. Find Dan's grade-school report card if you can.

as immoral smut peddlers. Concerned parents should not encourage politicians to cross the line into censorship by using their position in government to threaten and intimidate entertainment companies over their content. Free speechers would then be more comfortable supporting tools such as labels and filters that put control in the parent's hands.

CONSISTENCY
WINS CONSTITUENTS

[handwritten: Consistency is crazy, when you can't]

Conservatives have been able to build trust with consistency. Consistently articulating a simple, unchanging message signals an assuredness in what you're doing and where you're going. Yet they have to go to great lengths to appear consistent, because their "less government" principles clash with their general view of moral issues: Let's have as much government as possible to impose our moral beliefs on everyone else.

So instead of making honest arguments that will quickly lead to damning contradictions, they make disingenuous arguments that stay within their antigovernment framework. It's not that they want government to prevent women from choosing abortions and gays from getting married; it's that "liberal activist judges" want to impose their values on others. Never mind that no judge has ever tried to force a pregnant woman to get an abortion or a heterosexual to enter into a same-sex marriage. But such is the efficacy of consistency. It makes even dishonest arguments seem principled.

That's why it's important for us to take the time to root *all* of our positions in our set of core liberal principles, even for issues as disparate as gay rights, immigration, and fuel efficiency. A representative and responsive government that adheres to the will of the majority while preserving freedom for the minority. A responsible government that manages our resources wisely. A moral and pragmatic commitment to liberty and prosperity abroad.

And since we don't have to lubricate our arguments with snake oil in order to get our positions to fit together, we will be in a strong position to expose their fundamental hypocrisies and gain the moral high ground.

STAY AND FIGHT

Defuse the Culture War

✓Acknowledge and respect opposing views, so long as you don't violate your own principles in the process.

✓When discussing lifestyle and cultural issues, root your arguments in core liberal principles. For example, the pressure on our borders can be relieved if we renew our commitment to eradicating poverty abroad. Gays deserve the right to marry because a representative government cannot discriminate against some of its people. Our government should be responsive to our desire for higher fuel efficiency standards and responsibly manage our energy resources.

✓While consistently articulating liberal principles whenever you can, at the same time undermine the conservative attempt to appear principled. Point out how conservative leaders violate their own principles by railing against "big government" except when they want government to impose their beliefs on the personal decisions of others.

✓Put your money where your mouth is. Check out www.buyblue. org and learn what companies financially support the right-wing culture war.

CHAPTER 6

EXPRESS YOUR FAITH. OR NOT.

. . . the high level of religious activity in America compared to most other nations has been attributed by many experts to the high degree of separation between church and state. . . . The choice of faith is not coerced. . . . Families therefore feel a greater responsibility to . . . offer the faith leadership they believe is needed.

—Al and Tipper Gore

Is the "Christo-Fascist Zombie Brigade"—to quote Air America's Marc Maron—seeking salvation by gorging on our heathen liberal brains? Certainly an elite group of fringe fundamentalists *are* hell-bent on enshrining their interpretation of Christianity in our Constitution and laws. Beyond banning abortion and discriminating against gays and lesbians, they want to end stem-cell research, despite its promise to cure a range of diseases including diabetes and Parkinson's. They want "abstinence-only" programs in public schools, which worsen our public health by dishonestly disparaging contraception. They even want to cut funding for antidomestic violence programs that help women escape abusive relationships, because in their twisted view such programs don't support marriage.

When and how did this invasion happen? One of the most recent and disturbing instances was the Terri Schiavo controversy, when the notion of theocracy became a whole lot less theoretical.

The fundamentalist mob did not want to respect Schiavo's wishes and allow her life support to be removed because it violated their own religious views. And so they violated Schiavo's privacy. They sought to use the full weight of our federal government to project their beliefs onto one person's difficult moral decision. They pressured Republican leaders to ram through legislation giving the federal courts jurisdiction over the case, even though the local matter had been thoroughly litigated in the Florida courts. There even was a macabre attempt to subpoena Schiavo and her husband, bring them to Washington, and have them "testify" for a congressional investigation. Schiavo's wishes for a death on her terms were ultimately followed only because Republican-appointed federal judges refused to intervene, so severely shocking conservatives in Washington that they began sputtering about impeachments.

America was shocked as well—shocked to see such a brazen attempt to trample on personal freedom. Republicans were trying to legislate the views of right-wing Catholic and evangelical Protestant leaders, yet most American Catholics, most evangelical Protestants, most self-described conservatives, and most Americans overall opposed federal government intervention and supported the removal of Schiavo's feeding tube. The fringe fundamentalists showed how fringe they were.

For the health and safety of our communities, we desperately need to rally against this harmful agenda. And since none of those positions are backed by a majority of Americans, Democrats theoretically should have an easy time of it. Yet Democrats are increasingly hamstrung in attacking on this front, because there is a growing perception that they are hostile to religion. According to the Pew poll, the percentage of Americans who believe the party is "generally friendly toward religion" dropped from 40 percent in 2004 to 29 percent in 2005. (Though keep in mind that only 20 percent said Democrats were "unfriendly," while the rest said "neutral" or "didn't know." It's a brewing problem, not yet a full-blown disaster.)

Calling out the fringe fundamentalist agenda is decidedly not criticizing the entire religion of Christianity, nor is it attacking the right to share the fundamentalist belief that the Bible should be read literally. It's only opposing those religious leaders who, in league with the Republican Party, are trying to misuse our representative government to impose their beliefs on others. But those who suspect that Democrats are against religion will likely get the wrong impression when Democrats go after a small segment of Christianity. It won't matter whether that small segment is going after the rest of us.

So what can we do to reverse the perception that Democrats are antireligion, without surrendering the fight against the fringe fundamentalist political agenda?

MUST DEMOCRATS GET RELIGION?

Is the only way for Democrats and liberals to fight back the fundamentalist onslaught to wear religion on their sleeve and quote Bible scripture? Absolutely not. In fact, those who have been pushing Democrats in that direction often misstate and misread the poll data.

The Reverend Jim Wallis (a self-described "progressive" evangelical Christian), who has called for Democrats to "be much more willing to use moral and religious language in defense of economic fairness and justice," warned in February 2004 that Democrats have a "religion problem" because "[w]hile 63 percent of people who attend church more than once a week vote Republican, 62 percent of people who seldom or never attend vote Democratic."

But that's only a major problem if more voters attend religious services more than once a week than those that don't. The opposite is true. Only 16 percent of voters go to church more than once a week, while 42 percent go seldom or never. If you add in the people who go to church weekly, then there are an equal amount of voters who attend services at least weekly as there are voters who seldom or never go. It is true that regular churchgoers trend Republican and the "seldom or never" group trends Democratic, but that means you could just as easily say Republicans have a "secular problem."

Furthermore, Wallis didn't mention the 14 percent of voters who go to church monthly and make up a little analyzed swing group. Al Gore won those voters by five percentage points in 2000, and George W. Bush won them by one point in 2004—a shift more likely related to terrorism than anything religious in nature.

Similarly, *The Washington Monthly's* Amy Sullivan argued in a June 2003 article that Democratic candidates must tell voters "how faith informs their stances on issues such as health care and the environment." She bolstered her point by highlighting a poll that said "[s]eventy percent... want the president to be a person of faith." But Sullivan left out that the same poll found that 50 percent of Americans said "it makes me uncomfortable when politicians talk about how religious they are." Some voters (the poll data indicate about 20 percent) want both: a president who is a person of faith and doesn't browbeat you about it.

While Democrats do have a burgeoning perception problem when it comes to religion, the problem isn't as large (yet), and the solution isn't necessarily as simplistic, as Wallis, Sullivan, and others have made it. The Christian majority is nowhere near monolithic, and not all Christians insist upon having their elected representatives explicitly meld religious beliefs with policy positions.

But why ask me? I'm agnostic. (I do have faith that if God exists, He doesn't expect me to figure it all out while I'm alive.) I'm part of the 20 percent of the electorate that doesn't describe themselves as Christian, and part of the 42 percent that seldom or never goes to religious services. Who am I to say what religious voters want?

So I asked some.

WHAT DO MODERATE CHRISTIAN VOTERS WANT?

Through a churchgoing friend, I organized a discussion about religion and politics with several members of an evangelical Presbyterian church in North Carolina. The Presbyterian denomination is considered to be somewhat liberal. It backs abortion rights and supports some legal rights for gays and lesbians, but it does not support marriage rights for gays and will not ordain gay or straight single people who are unchaste. However, the evangelical faction is more conservative on social issues.

The group mostly consisted of self-described moderates, both registered Democrats and independents, who were reluctant John Kerry voters in 2004. Their opposition to the war or their support for antipoverty programs overrode their opposition to abortion. Or, as one said, "Kerry sucks less." They are regular churchgoers who attend a weekly Bible study group.

When I asked them whether they were looking for politicians to use more religious rhetoric, the answer was a clear no. They bristled at what they saw as insincere pandering and were far more interested in hearing more about politicians' core principles. To the extent that they appreciated a discussion of personal faith, it was to better understand those core principles. But no one, not even the more conservative people in the room who voted against Kerry, had a religious test for public office.

One woman said she wants candidates who are "true to themselves" and dislikes "the knee-jerk ubiquitous 'God Bless Yous' just to please an audience." She's frustrated that Democrats "don't understand Christians. They think they need to lay it on in the same manner as a Republican.... I'd rather just feel that the candidate does, in some way, good work...that's a reflection of his or her faith."

In that vein, another woman added:

> *I want to see Christian core values acted out...I want to see that in a politician's career.... Jimmy Carter was a really strong Christian...but he lived it rather than turning it into political rhetoric.... I'd probably rather just not hear it and see it instead.*

She defined "Christian core values" as simply "love, mercy, humility."

Yet another woman expressed deep disgust at "the way that Bush used religious rhetoric" during a 9/11 anniversary speech that implicitly described "America" as the "light of the world," which is how Jesus is described in the first chapter of John. "I think it's blasphemy to call a nation anything like Jesus. I would rather at that point have a president whose religious faith is somewhat hidden." And yet in general she is interested in knowing about a candidate's faith because "this idea that 'my religious beliefs don't influence my policy,' I don't understand that. I think people are shaped by core beliefs, and if you are a Christian, that will probably come out and that doesn't bother me."

At the same time, she is wide open to Christian candidates who are not as deeply devout as she is, as well as to non-Christians. She's happy with "a Muslim saying, 'My religious beliefs lead me to a compassion for the poor out of adherence to Allah.'" When asked if she's okay with a candidate whose core beliefs are not based on religion, she said yes, "as long as I think that they're being honest about that." She continued:

> *If it's kind of a, "I'm hiding my religious faith because I don't want people to think I mix the sacred and the secular," I'm going to be really skeptical of that. I'm going to bet that you do. . . . It's hard for me to imagine someone saying, "This is really central to me and yet it's not going to influence me."*
>
> *If you want to say, "I go to church on Sundays but really through the week I don't think about it much . . . and that's why it's not going to influence my decisions," I'd actually be more comfortable with that . . . Why not just say, "Look, at the end of the day, if I had to choose between the Bible and the Constitution, I'm for the Constitution." Just say that. . . . I want to know what finally is going to win.*

The two in the group who opposed Kerry made similar points about core principles ultimately being most important to them. One Bush voter was the only person who said he does want to hear religious rhetoric, but strictly in the pursuit of understanding core beliefs, not as a religious litmus test.

> *I believe everyone has a faith, everyone has a religion, that I would like to know about. Because that is a leading bearer on decisions, and policy decisions in particular, and that's what elections should be about. I would love to come out of*

an election season knowing the fundamentals upon which
a candidate made his decisions, because who knows what
issues are going to come up in the next 4 years.

When asked whether those fundamentals needed to be based in scripture, he said, "Not necessarily. . . . I think it's important for me as a voter to know where you're starting from. . . . In terms of religious rhetoric, any statement of core beliefs is that."

Meanwhile, a Libertarian Party supporter said, "I think it's important to identify what the core beliefs are . . . that determine everything else. And scripture can give you some of those core beliefs . . . but they wouldn't have to use scripture to convey the core beliefs that I'm looking for."

In short, weekly churchgoing Christians want candidates who are honest and sincere about their principles—just like any other voters.

SEPARATION OF CHURCH AND STATE IS NOT AN ALBATROSS

To erase the perception that liberals are against religion, is it necessary for us to keep quiet about our core belief that religious liberty is best protected by the constitutional separation of church and state? No. But it is true that unless we are working to end that perception, our discussion of church-state issues will feed it.

As we have seen, poll data about church-state issues reveal deeply mixed and even contradictory feelings. According to a 2004 Pew poll, 65 percent of people did not believe that churches should "come out in favor" of candidates, and 69 percent found it "improper" for political parties to procure church membership lists for get-out-the-vote purposes. But an even larger majority of 72 percent found it "proper" for the Ten Commandments to be displayed in government buildings, while a thin majority of 51 percent supported churches "express[ing] their views on day-to-day social and political questions."

At this point, the Ten Commandments issue has been resolved by the Supreme Court (it's okay if displayed in a historical context, not okay if displayed in a religious context). But it's a useful example to explore because it is the kind of issue that conservatives use against liberals. According to the poll data, that would appear to be smart strategy. In turn, it would appear to be smart strategy for liberals to just let such issues go and focus on other matters.

But my discussion with the North Carolina Christian group shows that there is more to that poll data than meets the eye. One of the reluctant Kerry backers said:

> *[Separation of church and state] was intended to protect people of faith and the church from interventions by the state. Of course, once a majority of a state becomes basically a certain church, then you need to protect the people who aren't in that church. . . . But it does leave a bad taste in my mouth when I see people whose primary mission is to eliminate—I just don't enjoy that. Doesn't make me feel good, even if I would maybe agree with them on whether or not the Ten Commandments should be in the Alabama courthouse.*

The hang-up is not the issue of separation of church and state itself. The hang-up is a perception that liberals are hostile to expressions of faith and want to use the First Amendment to quash them.

The key is to reverse that perception, not to compromise on liberal principles. How can we do that?

EXPRESSING FAITH SINCERELY

Simply put, Democrats should discuss honestly and openly how personal faith motivates them to achieve policy goals: whether faith influences them a lot, a little, or not at all. There is no need to tow a party line here. Sincerity is the best approach because it provides an authentic portrayal of a party, and a vision for America, where citizens of all backgrounds work side by side for the common good while protecting religious liberty for believers and nonbelievers—the essence of representative, responsible, and responsive government.

Granted, expressing personal faith can be easier said than done for Democratic candidates. Religion is an extremely thorny subject in our pluralistic society, with about 10 major denominations making up much of the Protestant majority, with Catholics constituting the biggest Christian denomination, with an evangelical movement cutting across Protestant denominations, and with about 20 percent of the country being non-Christians. And there is more religious diversity within the Democratic Party than the Republican Party, which is ultimately a party strength but also can lead to misunderstandings and division.

The best way to express one's faith without inappropriately signaling a desire for policies based solely on a specific interpretation of a religious text was described to me by the Rev. Barry Lynn, head of Americans United for Separation of Church and State. In an interview, he counseled that combining personal faith with secular reasoning is "the most authentic way to communicate." People of faith can express how their faith drives them to attain certain societal goals (i.e., "I'm personally committed to clothing the poor because I believe deeply in Jesus' teachings") while also offering secular-based reasons to persuade other Americans, believers and nonbelievers, to support specific policies (i.e., "More public investment in job training and college education for the poor will not only help those in need, but also enlarge our taxpayer base and grow our economy"). Says Rev. Lynn:

> *Nobody expects members of Congress to hang up their religion in the cloakroom before they go onto the floor, [but] they still must have a secular reason for . . . why they do or don't support a particular policy. [Otherwise, we'll see] dueling scripture verses on the floor of the House. . . .*
>
> *Most people can tell the difference between someone who is using a Bible verse solely as a justification for a policy vote, as a cover for that vote, and someone for whom this is simply one in a seamless set of arguments that leads to, what has to be in our system, a secular-based legal system.*

When candidates respect the distinction between personal faith and public rationales, the principle of church-state separation is not being compromised. If religious and nonreligious liberals fully embrace that effort, we can erase the false perception that liberalism is fundamentally hostile to religion.

STAY AND FIGHT

Express Your Faith. Or Not.

✓If you are religious, publicly discuss how your faith motivates you to fight for certain societal goals, such as health insurance for everyone, sufficient affordable housing, or an end to all forms of discrimination.

✓If you are not religious, be open with others about how your liberal ideals are rooted in your core beliefs and based on secular moral values.

✓Join the growing movement to revitalize the religious left. Check out new Christian organizations such as the Christian Alliance for Progress (christrianalliance.org) and CrossLeft (crossleft.org), or non-Christian groups like the Shalom Center (shalomctr.org), Tikkun (tikkun.org), and Muslim WakeUp! (muslimwakeup.com).

✓If you are Christian, find a church in your area through the Center for Progressive Christianity directory (tcpc.org/community) and get involved.

✓Participate in the religious blogosphere at sites such as Street Prophets (streetprophets.com), Father Jake Stops the World (frjakestopstheworld.blogspot.com), and A Religious Liberal Blog (religiousliberal.blogspot.com).

✓Fight fringe fundamentalist leaders at Talk to Action (talk2action.org) and Campaign to Defend the Constitution (defconamerica.org).

✓Listen to to Air America Radio's weekend religion shows, Saturday's *The Time Is Now* with The Reverend Dr. James A. Forbes, Jr. of the Riverside Church, and Sunday's *State of Belief* with The Reverend Dr. Welton Gaddy of the Interfaith Alliance.

DISROBE RIGHT-WING JUDGES

"Judicial activism will have to be deployed.... It's plain that the idea of judicial deference was a dead end for conservatives from the get-go."
—Michael Greve of the conservative American Enterprise Institute

Supreme Court politics are high-stakes and highly complex. The Court's jurisdiction is miles wide: schools and offices; corporations and workers; land, water, and air; race, religion, and gender; all of our fundamental rights and liberties. And since the nine Justices who make up the Court serve for life—as do the federal judges who sit on the less noticed but still influential lower courts—all judicial nominations by the President and confirmations by the Senate carry huge consequences felt by generations.

But most days you're probably not walking around thinking about how a Court ruling is affecting you. The language of judges and constitutional law is arcane, and the media generally does a terrible job translating it into layperson's terms. Talking about the Court in a fashion that most people would find relevant is difficult.

Yet right-wingers have had recent success in framing the ongoing judicial debate, mostly by skating past the issues involved. By characterizing conservative judges as those who "do not legislate from the bench," and by nominating those who come across as bland and reserved, Republicans are creating the impression that they want a nonthreatening, nonideological judiciary. They have also developed a negative label for liberal judges: "activists" who seek to impose their immoral values on an unwilling electorate.

Conversely, Democrats and liberals have not taken the time to adequately explain the difference between conservative and liberal judges. Instead, leading Democrats have tended to leave the impression that the only thing that matters in the Supreme Court debate is the issue of abortion. For example, the only mention of the Supreme Court in Al Gore's 2000 presidential nomination acceptance speech was, "The last thing this country needs is a Supreme Court that overturns Roe v. Wade."

Why is that a problem? After all, as we know, a clear majority of the country supports Roe.

Because the pro-Roe majority has not been as intense as the anti-Roe minority. More pro-Roe voters sided with George Bush than anti-Roe voters for Kerry in 2004. In a December 2005 *Washington Post* poll conducted during the Samuel Alito confirmation process, 61 percent said they wanted Alito to uphold Roe, but only 43 percent said it was "extremely" or "very" important that Alito agree with them on abortion.

Access to abortion affects way too many people for the issue to be downplayed or ignored. But the issue must be part of a larger framework, consistent with the liberal principle of representative, responsive, responsible government.

To build that framework, we have to fully understand how the conservative judicial activist agenda threatens liberal principles by establishing elitist government.

USING THE COURTS TO IMPOSE ONE VIEW OF MORALITY ON ALL

Control of the federal judiciary is of paramount importance to the power centers of the Republican Party: fringe fundamentalist religious leaders and crony corporate donors.

As noted in the previous chapter, the fringe fundamentalists want their particular interpretation of the Bible to be imposed on all other religious and nonreligious Americans. Their elitist vision for the Supreme Court would force women to carry out unwanted pregnancies, forbid terminally ill patients from having the choice to die with dignity, deny equal rights to gays and lesbians, and end religious liberty by supporting government-sponsored religion.

By complaining about "legislating from the bench," they cleverly present themselves as simple supporters of democracy and paint "activist liberal judges" as imposing their values on others. Of course, the opposite is true. Roe v. Wade does not force anyone to have an abortion, but overturning it will force women with unwanted pregnancies to bear children. Lawrence v. Texas does not force anyone to become gay, but overturning it would force gays to become criminals if they want to have sex. Engel v. Vitale does not prevent children of religious parents from praying wherever and whenever they like, but overturning it would force children of nonreligious parents to pray at the command of their public school teachers.

Those three landmark Supreme Court decisions—all of which have been attacked by current right-wing members of the Court—are classic liberal decisions. They rest on the liberal principle of representative government, ensuring that our government treats all Americans equally and protects everyone's freedom to make their own personal moral decisions. In contrast, a conservative judiciary would establish an elitist government that would impose one moral vision on all Americans.

Right-wingers insist that overturning such rulings will merely cede such moral matters to the states. That may be true at first, but that just means forced childbirth, forced heterosexuality, and forced prayer will happen in some parts of the country and not others. If you live in one of those states, it would make no difference that it's a state legislature and not a federal legislature robbing you of your freedoms.

Furthermore, don't think for a second that fringe fundamentalist leaders wouldn't try to pressure all 50 state legislatures, as well as the U.S. Congress, to pass laws imposing their religious views on others. They have already tried to bring the weight of the federal government down on Terri Schiavo. They're not even waiting for Roe to be overturned in South Dakota; in 2006, a law was enacted banning abortion even in cases of rape and incest. If the Supreme Court gives them the opportunity to leverage our government to intrude on more people's personal lives, they will run wild.

A GREEN LIGHT FOR BIG BUSINESS TO RUN AMOK

Meanwhile, the crony corporatists want the Court to grant them the ability to act irresponsibly and without accountability. *Business Week's* Lorraine Woellert laid plain this agenda when George W. Bush picked Samuel Alito for the Court, reporting that "Corporate America" breathed "a big sigh of relief" because "Alito ranked near the top for the boardroom set." What got them so excited?

In the 800-plus opinions he has penned during his 15 years as a federal judge, Alito consistently has come down on the side of limiting corporate liability, limiting employee rights, and limiting federal regulation. "He would be a liability restrainer," says Stan Anderson, legal-affairs lobbyist for the U.S. Chamber of Commerce.

To translate, if corporate executives want to pollute your community, sell you dangerous products, manipulate prices, squander your pension, shortchange your wages and benefits, or discriminate against female, minority, and disabled employees, they can usually count on conservative judges like Alito to shield them from accountability.

How? By denying citizens the right to bring cases to trial for a fair hearing, minimizing penalties on corporate lawbreakers, invalidating or weakening government regulations designed to stop bad corporate behavior, and even stripping the ability of your democratically elected Congress to pass laws that protect constitutional rights and promote the common good.

While conservative judges allegedly don't legislate from the bench, when they don't like the laws, they don't let Congress legislate either.

CONSERVATIVE JUDGES: THE REAL ACTIVISTS

In fact, Yale Law professor Paul Gewirtz and Yale Law graduate Chad Golder analyzed how Supreme Court justices voted when Congressional laws and provisions came before them. After sifting through all the relevant rulings between 1994 and 2005, a period when the composition of the Court remained unchanged, they reported in a New York Times op-ed that the four justices typically deemed liberal were the ones who "least frequently" voted to strike down federal laws, and the opposite was true for the conservatives. They concluded: "At least by this measure . . . the [conservative] group is the most activist."

How big is the activist gap between conservative and liberal justices? The most conservative member of the Court, Clarence Thomas, was also the most activist, striking down Congressional provisions 66 percent of the time. The two justices appointed by a Democratic president—Stephen Breyer and Ruth Bader Ginsburg—were at the bottom of the activist list, overruling Congress 28 percent and 39 percent of the time, respectively.

What kinds of laws have already been wiped off the books by conservative justices? There are two notable instances from the era of Chief Justice William Rehnquist, who presided over the Court from 1986 to 2005. One, in 1995, erased a law banning guns within 1,000 feet of a school. Another, in 2000, weakened the Violence Against Women Act by denying rape victims and other victims of domestic and sexual violence the ability to take their attackers to federal court.

Both of these rulings were decided on a 5–4 vote along ideological lines and appeased elements of the conservative movement.

The demise of "Gun Free School Zones" obviously satisfied the libertarian extremists that lead the gun lobby. Less obviously, fringe fundamentalist leaders were pleased to see efforts to combat domestic violence and sexual assault taken down a peg. Concerned Women for America (CWFA), a conservative group that claims to "bring Biblical principles into all levels of public policy," has attacked the Violence Against Women Act (VAWA), as have fellow ideological travelers the Heritage Foundation and the intentionally misnamed Independent Women's Forum.

The Cybercast News Service (original name: Conservative News Service) interviewed CWFA's Wendy Wright and reported: "According to Wright, VAWA 'has become a huge funneling scheme to radical feminist activists who use the funding to basically set up antimen programs. . . . Women are not always the victim; they are sometimes the perpetrators of violence.'" (For the record, this "huge funneling scheme" that supports shelters, treatment, and education led to a 50 percent drop in nonfatal domestic violence and a 20 percent drop in fatal domestic violence. True, the victims weren't all women—just 85 percent of them.) CWFA also praised John Roberts when he was nominated to the Supreme Court in part because of his stated animosity to the law.

What's the connection to "Biblical principles"? Marriage. Concerned Women for America argues that "[t]he institution of marriage represents more than a private, individual choice. The deterioration of marriage affects the safety of women and children, indeed, all of society[,]" ergo "marriage offers the best protection against violence toward women and children." The Violence Against Women Act (which passed in part because of the advocacy of the feminist organization Legal Momentum, where I once served as Deputy Communications Director) has the nerve to presume that victimized women need help to escape abusive relationships, married or otherwise, when from the right-wing perspective all you need to stop those beatings is to just say "I do."

The import of these two cases goes beyond the specific issues of school shootings and domestic violence. The reasoning used by the conservative members of the Court set a precedent that struck a blow against the very essence of our democracy: the people's right to have their Congress pass laws that help solve national problems.

In an August 2005 address to the Los Angeles County Bar Association, Democratic senator Dianne Feinstein said that in the 10 years following the Gun Free School Zones ruling,

the Rehnquist Court has continued this restrictive, some might say "activist," position. Its decisions have wholly or partially invalidated more than three dozen federal statutes in the past 10 years. . . . They include: the Brady Handgun Violence Protection Act, which seeks to keep guns out of the hands of criminals; the Age Discrimination in Employment Act, and the Americans with Disabilities Act, both of which seek to protect citizens from discrimination.

The newest additions to the Court had taken Rehnquist's cues as lower court judges. In 2003, John Roberts sought to apply the gun-free zones and sexual violence rulings to justify a severe limitation of our government's power to save endangered species in our ecosystems. Similarly, Sam Alito voted in 1996 to prevent Congress from being able to ban machine guns, in an attempted expansion of the gun-free zones decision. (Both Roberts and Alito were outvoted by their more independent lower-court peers.)

How far-reaching is the potential of this conservative judicial activist philosophy embodied in these two key rulings of the Rehnquist Court? As constitutional scholar Cass Sunstein has written, it could hold that Congress is forbidden to create offices that protect the environment, prosecute crooked stock traders, and resolve labor disputes fairly. It could undermine Social Security, scrap antidiscrimination laws, block campaign finance reform, and repeal any minimum wage.

MASKING THEIR AGENDA WITH DUPLICITY, EVASION, AND INCREMENTALISM

Having said that, keep in mind that the conservative movement is not stupid. They understand that the public is not supportive of such a radical philosophy. So when conservative Supreme Court nominees come before the Senate, they don't candidly lay out their philosophy and subject it to open debate. They evade questions about their judicial views as much as possible, and when evasion doesn't cut it, they mislead. This strategy is known as "confirmation conversion."

Justice Antonin Scalia, when asked at his hearing whether he would overturn Roe since he had previously said abortion was "no business" of the courts, replied, "I assure you I have no agenda." He later voted to overturn it. He also contended he would give great deference to the Congress, telling Senators, "You write it, and I'll enforce it." Once on the Court, he sided with the 5–4 majority in the two milestone cases on gun-free zones and sexual violence that curtailed Congressional power.

Justice Clarence Thomas said in his confirmation hearings that he would have an "open mind" about Roe, and that the principle of respecting past Court precedents was "critical" and "very important." Less than one year later he joined fellow prevaricator Scalia in an anti-Roe dissent. (In 2006, Alito echoed Thomas when he said in his hearings that he would have an "open mind" on abortion cases.)

Chief Justice John Roberts won the vote of Senator Ron Wyden of Oregon by leading the Senator to believe he would respect Oregon's law allowing physician-assisted suicide. In August 2005, *The Oregonian's* Jim Barnett reported:

> **Supreme Court nominee John Roberts declared that, in cases dealing with end-of-life care, he would "start with the supposition that one has the right to be left alone," Sen. Ron Wyden, D-Ore., said after the two met for an hour Tuesday. . . . Roberts told Wyden that he would look closely at the**

legislative history of federal laws and would be careful not to strip states of powers they traditionally have held—such as regulating the practice of medicine, Wyden said.

In one of Roberts' first votes after being confirmed, he supported the authority of then–U.S. Attorney General John Ashcroft to arbitrarily invalidate the Oregon law, despite the absence of any federal law banning assisted suicide.

The craftiness of conservatives does not end with the confirmation process. They are well aware that a wholesale whitewash of constitutional protections and an abrupt strangulation of Congressional power could spark a massive backlash. So they proceed pragmatically and stealthily.

Chief Justice Roberts will likely follow in the footsteps of his predecessor Rehnquist and be calculating with regard to the sweep of Court opinions (Rehnquist was also a mentor to Roberts, one of his former law clerks). For example, in a 2001 case involving the Clean Water Act, Rehnquist didn't go through the trouble of overturning the law to get the desired anti-environmental result. He simply negated the regulation that the Army Corps of Engineers used to enforce the law and protect bodies of water serving as habitat for migratory birds. The Clean Water Act stays on the books, but in weakened form.

Rehnquist's pragmatism extended beyond restraining his own conservative colleagues. In 2003, when the Court was ruling whether Congress could mandate state governments to grant their employees family and medical leave, Rehnquist realized he didn't have the votes to rule against Congress. So he switched sides and joined the majority. That gave him the power, as Chief Justice, to write the majority opinion, and he was able to limit the damage the case did to his long-term goal of constraining Congressional power.

As liberals, what do we do with our understanding of the conservative agenda and judiciary strategy?

PORTRAY TWO CONTRASTING VISIONS FOR OUR JUDICIARY

We must succinctly portray the dark vision of what a conservative judiciary will eventually bring about—an elitist government, no longer representative of and responsive to its people, handcuffed from insisting upon responsible corporate behavior, but free to subject all Americans to one group's version of morality.

At the same time we should compare that dark conservative vision with a positive liberal vision. We must reject any notion that a liberal judiciary would be similarly activist, which would wrongly suggest that landmark liberal Supreme Court rulings were not in line with both the text and spirit of our Constitution. Instead, we should explicitly emphasize how liberalism is the best defender of the Constitution. In our view, judges are the ones who should maintain the representative and responsive government envisioned by our Founders: allowing us to pass laws that promote the common good; protecting our freedom to make private, moral decisions; and giving all citizens equal access and impartial treatment in the courthouse.

We must be careful to paint a realistic picture of what can be expected in the foreseeable future. If we offer a hyperbolic vision that does not materialize after a few years, we will lose credibility and conservatives will be free to continue their slow, incremental march on the Constitution.

The best way to stay rooted in reality is to call attention to real actions by the Roberts Court, and by lower court judges, that can illuminate the path that the right-wing wants to put us on, not only when conservative majorities set troubling precedents but also when conservatives come out on the short end of 5–4 votes (which may still happen, so long as a swing vote on the Court remains). Because the conservative movement is in the catbird's seat, it's more important to take advantage of any opportunity to articulate the dangers of a conservative judiciary than to praise a temporary pause in its trajectory.

This is easier said than done for most individuals because the significance of cases isn't always obvious on the surface—at first blush, you wouldn't know that the Gun Free School Zones and Violence Against Women cases are fundamentally about your ability to have Congress pass beneficial legislation. Solely relying on the mainstream media to understand the larger relevance of Court actions is not recommended because reporters often mischaracterize rulings by way of oversimplification. Liberal legal organizations tend to have the opposite problem: an inability to explain cases without getting bogged down in jargon. For helpful, plainspoken analysis, blogs are a better bet. Quality legal blogs include acsblog.org, balkin.blogspot.com, glenngreenwald.blogspot.com, isthatlegal.org, and lefarkins.blogspot.com.

SETTING THE BAR FOR FUTURE NOMINEES

If we succeed in raising red flags about a conservative judiciary, we will be in a far better position to fight conservative nominees than we were when Roberts and Alito were nominated.

The burden should be on the nominees to prove—based primarily on their past records, not on their "confirmation conversions"—that they do not hold a conservative judicial philosophy. While it is inappropriate to ask nominees how they would vote on future cases, it is entirely appropriate for nominees to share their views on the philosophy of past Supreme Court rulings. Any attempts to avoid answering substantive questions should be disqualifying. The bar for lifetime appointments should not be set so low that nominees who lack a paper record of their judicial views, or who give evasive and misleading answers to questions about their views, are waived through.

Unfortunately, the bar was set too low in 2005 and 2006 for the Roberts and Alito nominations to the Court.

In the case of Roberts, Democrats and liberal civil rights groups hadn't thought through how to oppose a nominee who didn't have a significant paper trail. So they generally remained quiet as Republicans relentlessly spun how "brilliant" Roberts was. Without any opposition putting up a fight and making an argument about why not to accept a blank slate for a lifetime appointment, Roberts skated.

Alito had more of a record for opponents to work with, but the *Washington Post* reported at the conclusion of his hearings, "When the hearings began . . . liberal activists said their best hope was for Alito to commit a gaffe or lose his composure." That's a very easy bar to clear, so long as you offer lots of platitudes and restrain yourself from screaming out, "Oh, will you shut up already, Joe Biden?!"

With even the opposition setting a low bar, the media followed suit. When Alito was systematically evasive on key questions, the media treated that as praiseworthy, not suspicious. During the hearings, the *Chicago Tribune* wrote that "Alito has succeeded in deflecting attacks and avoiding major blunders, turning in a solid if not dazzling performance, and seems headed toward confirmation." CNN offered that "this has been a cakewalk for Samuel Alito so far," and "the judge has pretty much breezed through the issues."

Yes, the Supreme Court is a government institution that can

seem far removed from daily life, but if we fail to stoke concern about what conservative judges have up their sleeves, then even winning back the White House and the Congress may not be enough to stop the right-wing from achieving their antifreedom agenda.

STAY AND FIGHT

Disrobe Right-Wing Judges

✓Insist that conservative judges are *activists:* Their agenda is to handcuff our government from promoting responsible corporate behavior—such as protecting our rivers or providing safe workplaces—while permitting a select group of extremist religious leaders to impose their version of morality on all Americans.

✓Tout the advantages of a liberal judiciary: maintaining representative and responsive government; allowing us to establish programs that promote the common good, such as Social Security, the minimum wage, and the Violence Against Women Act; protecting our freedom to make private, moral decisions through rulings such as Roe; and giving all citizens equal access and impartial treatment in the courthouse.

✓Pressure your Senators to aggressively challenge future nominees to prove they are not conservative judicial activists.

✓Point out now—well in advance of future nominations—to anyone and everyone who will listen, how judicial rulings affect Americans. Keep track of this yourself by regularly reading political blogs such as LiberalOasis.com to stay on top of legal rulings and their short-term and long-term consequences.

CHAPTER 8

ENGAGE THE CORPORATE MEDIA

"People cannot govern what they cannot see."
—James Squires, former *Chicago Tribune* Washington bureau chief

When the Fairness Doctrine was repealed by President Ronald Reagan in 1987, removing the mandate on broadcast outlets to give equal time to opposing political views, conservatives led by Rush Limbaugh jumped at the chance to get behind the mic and spread the conservative word. Liberals at first saw no use for the medium, thinking that it offered only unreasoned, one-sided rants. But conservatives understood that talk radio allowed audience members to find their voices as well. It wasn't about being yelled at. It was about sharing ideas and information (or misinformation, as is the case for many conservative hosts) in a public way. It was about fostering a grassroots community that could speak much louder collectively than its members could individually—loud enough to influence the rest of the media landscape.

Seventeen years later, liberals finally figured out that we could not have an effective voice in today's media environment without a similar network, and Air America Radio was born. Despite naysaying that there wasn't a market for liberal talk, in 2 years Air America expanded from 6 stations to more than 80.

Far from offering cookie-cutter diatribe 24-7, each Air America show quickly developed its own style and focus, ensuring that fans could listen all day and be continually enlightened, entertained, and energized. Al Franken, who anchors the network in the 12:00-to-3:00 P.M. slot, delivers a dry wit and steady flow of A-list guests from Washington. Randi Rhodes rips through the afternoon drive time, as quick with her facts as she is with her putdowns. In the evening, comedians Janeane Garofalo and Sam Seder artfully weave biting satire with thought-provoking commentary while sharing their microphones with artists, activists, and bloggers like myself— every Monday night, I break down the Sunday morning political talk shows with analysis that isn't regurgitated from Washington cocktail party chatter.

But while the creation of a vibrant national liberal media outlet with the long reach of radio is an important step forward, its mere existence does not fix the sorry state of the mainstream media, which is a major obstacle to achieving a liberal America. We can't make informed decisions about the role of our government, the proper level of taxation, and the goals of our foreign policy if the national media disproportionately focuses on sensationalized local crime stories and reflexively reiterates White House statements.

THE END OF JOURNALISM AS WE KNEW IT?

It is said that the media is the fourth branch of government. In reality, the media is a business. If media industry executives concluded that functioning as a public service would yield profits, then we'd get more thorough reporting on international matters. We'd have a

brighter spotlight on the struggles of our nation's poor and unin-
sured. We'd see a greater willingness to note when our leaders make
misleading remarks. We'd find a stronger reliance on real experts,
not phony experts who are actually pseudo-academic political operatives. And we wouldn't see political hit groups like the Swift Boat
Veterans for Truth get air time unless and until reporters deter-
mined that their information was credible.

We don't have a media motivated by public service. We have a
media motivated by profit. And while media outlets were always
commercial enterprises, it is only in recent history that most of our
media has been owned by bottom-line-driven corporate conglomer-
ates, not by individual media barons who were more tolerant of small
profits.

Former *Chicago Tribune* Washington bureau chief James Squires,
in his book *Read All About It! The Corporate Takeover of America's
Newspapers*, summed up the consequences of this shift in owner-
ship: "Rather than educating and challenging citizens, the press's
purpose has become attracting and entertaining consumers. . . ."

And in October 2002, in an address at Middle Tennessee State
University, former Vice President Al Gore noted that TV networks
"have had to add something extra to their news broadcasts," as news
has become a commodity, thus damaging the quality of reporting. In
Gore's words as reported by the student newspaper *Sidelines Online*,
that means "news plus entertainment, news plus attitude, news plus
opinion." Because they are under pressure to break news, networks
even "run pre-written pieces" making "themselves vulnerable to . . .
prepackaged and preprocessed facts according to a particular point
of view."

Not fact checking, not adding details, not bothering to put spoon-
fed information in proper context—basically, not practicing traditional journalism—has another benefit beyond speed: It saves money.
Paying a guy to dole out opinions every night is much cheaper than

paying a team of reporters to investigate a potential story over the course of weeks. For example, according to the 2006 State of the Media report from the Project for Excellence in Journalism, Fox News's expenses are $200 million less than CNN's, and it operates 21 fewer international bureaus than CNN. Perhaps it's not surprising, then, that the University of Maryland's Program on International Policy Attitudes (PIPA) found that the Fox News audience, which tends to be conservative, has been far more misinformed about the Iraq War than any other audience. Yet Fox consistently, and handily, beats CNN in the prime-time ratings and turns a healthy profit. (CNN has a larger overall audience and is more profitable than Fox, but Fox has been closing the profit gap.)

The October 2003 PIPA study found that 80 percent of Fox News watchers had at least one factual misperception about the Iraq War, such as that the United States found evidence that Saddam Hussein was working closely with Al Qaeda, or that the United States found weapons of mass destruction in Iraq. But that doesn't exonerate the rest of the corporate media: 71 percent of CBS watchers were similarly misinformed, 61 percent for ABC, 55 percent for NBC and CNN, and 47 percent for print media readers. Pretty poor marks across the board.

What can be done to fix this pathetic situation so we can finally have the kind of public-service media we need for a functioning representative democracy? We need to take our status as news consumers seriously and demand better from the media corporations.

HOW CONSERVATIVES ENGAGE THE MAINSTREAM MEDIA

Rather than fight the appalling lameness of most mainstream media, some of us have taken the path of least resistance: tuning out the corporate media and turning to more "intellectual" media such as National Public Radio and the Public Broadcasting System (NPR and PBS watchers scored best in the PIPA study, with only 23 percent holding at least one Iraq War misconception), or the *New York Times*.

But shunning the mainstream media has done nothing to raise the bar. It has simply created a small cocoon of relatively better-informed citizens. As many as 13 million Americans tune in to NPR's *Morning Edition*, and 8 million watch PBS's *The NewsHour with Jim Lehrer* each week. About 14 million read the *Times* or go to NYTimes.com each month. Those are healthy numbers considering how splintered our media landscape has become. But it's still a fraction of the population—and keep in mind that there is surely significant overlap between those three audiences.

Of course, conservatives have created their own network of media to rely on, including Fox News, the Drudge Report, and an army of right-wing talk radio hosts.

The difference is that these conservative news consumers have not created a cocoon. They are not lulled into passivity with soft jazz intros and dulcet-toned news readers. They take the talking points that are blasted by Bill O'Reilly and Rush Limbaugh and thrust them upon traditional media outlets in hopes of altering the news coverage for the rest of the country.

A notable example of this tactic is the pressure campaign for the mainstream media to report more "good news" from Iraq.

In the summer of 2003 the Iraq War took a bad turn as the insurgency began to form and bombings rattled the country. Bush's approval ratings weakened as a result. On August 25, 2003, Defense Secretary Donald Rumsfeld sounded the call to blame the media for simply reporting on the violence:

With 24-hour news, each setback in Iraq is repeated and repeated and repeated as if it were 10 or 20 setbacks. And the progress that's being made—and let there be no doubt, solid progress is being made—is often not deemed sufficiently newsworthy to report.

Conservative pundits responded to the call and stepped up their attacks on the media.

The September 1, 2003, issue of the right-wing *National Review* magazine berated "the antiwar movement and its media accomplices" for trying to make the war appear "unwinnable" by "keep[ing] the actual details of what is happening there rather vague."

On September 10, 2003, *The Wall Street Journal* ran an op-ed by a Fellow at the conservative American Enterprise Institute think tank, claiming that

We...have been at the mercy of images presented to us by the press. We all know that journalists have a bad-news bias: 10,000 schools being rehabbed is not news; one school blowing up is a weeklong feeding frenzy. And some of us who have spent time recently in Iraq...have been puzzled by the postwar news and media imagery, which is much more negative than what many individuals involved in reconstructing Iraq have been telling us.

And Fox News commentator Fred Barnes complained on the September 24, 2003, edition of *Special Report with Brit Hume*:

It's a bad-news bias.... It's something that infects the press and it certainly does in Baghdad. Everybody I have talked to, whether it's military personnel or journalists who have gone over [to Iraq], said the same thing. And that is that the mainstream press is reporting a much more negative situation than actually exists in Baghdad. That things are

gradually getting better there. The U.S. is doing well....
This idea that the U.S. is losing the postwar is completely
wrong.

Partisan pundits toeing the party line is nothing unusual. What is unusual is the grassroots activity that followed. E-mails of undetermined origin began to circulate in late 2003, chronicling supposed accomplishments in Iraq that the media allegedly wasn't telling the public about. One of these e-mails said:

DID YOU KNOW THIS?

Did you know that 47 countries have re-established their embassies in Iraq?

Did you know that the Iraqi government employs 1.2 million Iraqi people?

Did you know that 3,100 schools have been renovated, 364 schools are under rehabilitation, 263 schools are now under construction, and 38 new schools have been built in Iraq?...

OF COURSE WE DIDN'T KNOW!

WHY DIDN'T WE KNOW? OUR MEDIA WOULDN'T TELL US!

Because a Bush-hating media and Democratic Party would rather see the world blow up than lose their power.

But these e-mails didn't just circulate among fellow conservatives. For the next few years, reporters were bombarded with such e-mails.

The pressure tactic seems to have worked. According to *The New York Times*, a July 2005 meeting was held between newspaper editors and the Associated Press, the nonprofit news agency that feeds stories to 1,700 papers. The newspaper editors, prompted by the specific e-mail above, questioned the AP about whether it was properly reporting what was happening in Iraq. One *Tampa Tribune* editor said afterward, "People wanted to know if we're making progress in Iraq. . . . There's a perception that we're not telling the whole story."

The right-wing media would not be this influential if its audience were not so actively engaged. The one-two punch of the Beltway conservative elite and the conservative grassroots, casting themselves as the voice of middle America and pounding on the traditional media establishment, has made mainstream reporters and editors second-guess themselves.

But is there any evidence that the liberal grassroots can similarly influence corporate media outlets? In fact, there is.

After the 2004 presidential election there were reports of election irregularities in Ohio, but since John Kerry conceded, the national media decided not to bother exploring the story. The lone exception was Keith Olbermann, the host of MSNBC's 8:00 P.M. weeknight show, *Countdown*, who discussed the alleged irregularities for 15 minutes on the Monday after Election Day.

Immediately, MSNBC received enormous positive feedback from its audience. By 10:30 that night it had received 1,508 thankful e-mails and only 62 critical ones. Olbermann noted on his blog the next day: "the volume [of e-mail] is startling. . . . I know some of the overtly liberal [web]sites encouraged readers to write, but that's still a hunk of mail, and a decisive margin."

A flood of negative e-mail would have put pressure on Olbermann and his bosses to cease pursuing the story, fearing not only a short-term drop in ratings but also long-term damage to the network brand. MSNBC had previously shown its willingness to fire people for fear of being called a liberal network. Just before the start of the

Iraq War, MSNBC cancelled *Donahue,* its highest-rated program at the time, after an internal study expressed concern that the antiwar host Phil Donahue would be a "difficult public face for NBC in a time of war" and that the show could become "a home for the liberal antiwar agenda at the same time that our competitors are waving the flag at every opportunity."

The positive e-mail following the Ohio election report helped to contain any similar fears, and Olbermann's reports continued up until the Congress was forced to formally debate the irregularities before approving the Electoral College results. Supportive e-mails kept pouring in—on November 21, Olbermann blogged: "I've gotten 37,000 e-mails in the last 2 weeks (now running at better than 25:1 in favor)." Most importantly, ratings improved. MSNBC's prime-time ratings in the key 25- to 54-year-old demographic were up 78 percent in November 2004 compared with November 2003. And the ratings increase for *Countdown,* 128 percent, was the largest of any show in MSNBC's prime-time lineup.

Of course, this one effort did not transform MSNBC and other outlets into aggressive, hard-news operations that do not cower in the face of "liberal bias" attacks. To realize such an ambitious goal, a sustained and broad engagement of the corporate media is needed.

DON'T COPY
THE CONSERVATIVES

What should this engagement look like? Should we replicate the conservative strategy and loudly whine whenever anything is said that doesn't serve our interests? No, if for no other reason than it wouldn't do anything to change the media for the better.

"There's an old adage in journalism that if both sides attack you, then you must be doing something right," said *The Washington Post* recently in defense of one of its reporters. This is false comfort: One side's criticism may have merit and the other side's may not. Nevertheless, that is the defensive, stubborn reaction that we will receive from the media if we simply ape the right wing's approach.

To ensure that our message isn't shrugged off, we must be careful not to attack the media on political grounds. Instead, we should play to what's left of journalistic pride. We need to make clear that our goal is not a media that chooses political sides but one that puts out a good product and ably informs the public. We must stress that unlike the right wing, we are supporters of a strong, vibrant media. We seek to enhance the media's ability to speak truth to power, not render it submissive to those in power. Our fundamental message to the media is not "stop conservative bias." It's "stop shoddy journalism."

And to carry that message, our engagement with the corporate media should fall under the following three categories.

1. Calling Attention to Underreported Stories. It is the job of reporters and editors to judge the day's events and decide which are the most newsworthy. Part of their calculation is, "What will be of interest to our readers?" They can't make good calculations unless we tell them what we're interested in.

That's essentially what happened with the Ohio election story. After Olbermann went against the collective news judgment of every other national news editor, a segment of the public responded and said they wanted to hear more. MSNBC obliged and scored in the ratings.

Blogs have the shown some ability to call attention to underreported scandals, such as when Eschaton (atrios.blogspot.com) and Talking Points Memo (talkingpointsmemo.com) hammered Senator Trent Lott for claiming that America would have been better off if Strom Thurmond's 1948 segregationist presidential bid had been victorious. The comments, which initially aired on C-SPAN and were first reported on ABC News's web-only feature *The Note*, likely would have slipped through the cracks if those blogs hadn't indicated that people were livid at Lott's remarks.

But scandals aren't the only things that are underreported. There is scant coverage of American poverty. There is little analysis of foreign policy geared to laymen or free from influence by those pushing agendas. The amount of reporting on the policy views of political candidates pales in comparison with the ink spilled trying to determine who is "up" and who is "down" in the horse race. The paucity of hard news leads to an electorate that is less informed, less aware of the problems our society faces, less knowledgeable of what solutions are available, and less connected to their representative government.

How can we best communicate to media representatives that we, the consumers, want more substantive journalism, less sensationalism, less fluff, and no kowtowing to our public servants?

As with Olbermann's Ohio election story, we should send in positive feedback. Read something halfway decent on page 23 of your local paper? Contact the reporter (or the reporter's editor if you are able to identify who that is) and say things like, "Good work," "Please continue reporting on this story in greater detail," "Give it a higher profile," or "Have you considered additional coverage from this perspective?" Never underestimate the power of flattery.

Another approach is to try to fan the flames of a good story beyond its origin. For example, after seeing a well-reported article in your local paper, drop an e-mail to your local TV or radio station and encourage it to further explore the issue. Or you can play on the competitive nature of news organizations, calling one cable TV channel and pointedly asking why it failed to cover a certain story that one of its rivals did.

How do you know exactly whom to contact? For most media

outlets, it isn't too hard to obtain an e-mail address or phone number of a specific reporter from the receptionist. Some newspapers publish reporters' e-mails at the bottom of their articles. Tracking down editors can be trickier. Your best bet is to call the front desk, tell the operator the message you want to send, then ask which editor it would be best to send it to. Many major media companies have an ombudsman who is tasked with relaying what is on consumers' minds to the editorial leadership.

And whenever you contact members of the media—whether you do it by mail, e-mail, or phone—always remember that while they are often interested in hearing feedback, they are also constantly pressed for time. Keep your communications succinct and polite. Long essays will be ignored and angry rants will be dismissed.

2. Correcting Misinformation. Conservatives have become quite deft at injecting misinformation into the media bloodstream. For instance, in recent years they have said that Ruth Bader Ginsburg did not answer questions about her views of past Supreme Court rulings in her confirmation hearings, that African-Americans get less out of Social Security than whites, and that Ambassador Joe Wilson claimed that Vice President Dick Cheney directly sent him to Niger, just to name a few.

Because conservatives have their own media infrastructure of Web sites and talk-radio shows, it is difficult for us to stop all misinformation at its source. But we can disrupt its flow if we recognize it quickly and call attention to it.

Of course, it's not easy for even a well-informed individual to spot misinformation on his or her own. Fortunately, there is an organization that provides people with the necessary tools. Media Matters for America specializes in "rapid-response" media criticism, and its MediaMatters.org Web site is a massive operation, scouring every inch of the TV, radio, print, and Internet media landscape and constantly correcting conservative misinformation. Every item Media Matters posts includes contact information for the media outlet that erred, so users can easily press editors to make amends.

And they have had successes. For example, on September 4, 2005, *The Washington Post* reported that the Louisiana governor had yet to declare a state of emergency nearly a week after the storm, citing an anonymous "senior Bush official" as the source. That was demonstrably false. The governor declared a state of emergency on August 26, 3 days before the storm—information that was easily verifiable on the state government Web site. After Talking Points Memo pointed out the misinformation, the *Post* ran a correction. But it was a terse correction that failed to acknowledge how the error came about, implying that it was a run-of-the-mill slip-up on the part of the paper and not the result of a presidential aide trying to dishonestly shift blame to state officials under the cover of anonymity that the *Post* provided.

Media Matters then posted an open letter to the *Post's* ombudsman, Michael Getler, criticizing the original story and the correction. That prompted the ombudsman, in his weekly column, to provide a fuller explanation of what happened and knock the paper for "the inadequacy of the correction." Getler noted the role of Media Matters readers in getting his attention, writing, "The incident produced hundreds of critical e-mails, many of them undoubtedly provoked by a critique by Media Matters for America."

It actually doesn't take that much—several hundred e-mails making a solid argument—to pressure a media outlet into making amends. But making amends is only half the battle. As the saying goes, "A lie is halfway around the world before the truth has got its boots on." Getting the correction published may help diminish the repetition of misinformation, but ideally we want to prevent misinformation in the first place. That means contacting traditional media outlets *before* the lies reach them.

It is impractical for an individual to contact every traditional outlet in the nation every time the Right pushes out a dose of inaccurate spin. (Blast e-mails to large lists are routinely ignored by recipients and can cause your e-mail address to get blocked.) More feasible is for individuals to adopt a national, state, or local news outlet and regularly contact an ombudsman or news editor there to alert them to specific misinformation that's in the pipeline.

E-mail is the best method of communication for this task—editors likely would not appreciate phone calls regarding an item that they haven't yet published or aired, and regular mail is too slow to beat the speed of lies. Again, keep your e-mails short and polite. If your e-mails are readable and useful, you will establish yourself as a credible source of information and editors won't instinctually click "Delete" at the mere sight of your e-mail address.

3. Encouraging Aggressive Questioning. Your average modern TV interview is mainly an opportunity for a politician to disseminate precooked talking points, as interviewers mostly lob softball questions. Even when the occasional hardball question is asked, guests often slip past them because interviewers rarely bother with follow-up questions.

Why is this so? Corporate media executives worry that rough-and-tumble questioning will make it harder to book A-list guests and lead to lower ratings.

In the January/February 2004 issue of *Columbia Journalism Review*, Trudy Lieberman explored this phenomenon:

> **One media trainer [a person who teaches politicians and business executives how to handle media interviews] says**

that in the time of Edward R. Murrow and Fred Friendly,
journalists could bully their guests because they knew CBS
was behind them. "They can't be as abusive as they used to
be," she says.

So unwritten rules now dictate acceptable behavior.
Ask questions too harshly, and you're outside the club. . . .
Bob Schieffer [host of CBS's Face the Nation*] explains, "You*
don't want to appear rude even though the guest can be
filibustering and killing time, and you can't ask what you
want." Schieffer's colleague Steve Hartman says interview-
ers must be careful not to cut the guest off too soon or
"you're going to be perceived as someone who has a bias.
Everyone is concerned about how they come across in this
game."

How can we disrupt this dynamic? By regularly sending the message to talk-show hosts and producers that their audiences would
grow if questioning were more aggressive and extracted more information with less spin.

A good area to focus on is Sunday-morning talk. NBC's *Meet the
Press*, CBS's *Face the Nation*, ABC's *This Week*, and CNN's *Late Edition* are interview shows that are faithfully watched by the political
and media establishment, and they can set the tone for the week
ahead. Most weeks, the shows' Web sites announce who the Sunday
guests will be on Friday afternoon. And the Web sites invite viewers
to send in suggestions.

So, make it a habit every Friday evening or Saturday morning to
submit three tough and thoughtful questions you would like to see
asked of a particular guest. And always add a reminder that you
would appreciate a follow-up question if the guest tries to dodge the
question.

If you're not a regular viewer of the Sunday shows because you find the endless, unchecked spin tiresome, say so. While submitting your questions, tell the shows that you normally don't watch but that if you see the questioning become more pointed and illuminating, you'll become a regular viewer. Such a message may be particularly effective with the shows that are lagging in the ratings (at this writing, NBC's *Meet the Press* has been the ratings leader for several years, frustrating executives at CBS and ABC.)

DON'T LET *THE NEW YORK TIMES* AND NPR OFF THE HOOK

The call to engage the media does not exclude supposedly liberal outlets such as *The New York Times* and National Public Radio. Yes, they may be relatively better at providing public service than the rest of the corporate media, but they have proven susceptible to the same right-wing pressures that other media outlets face.

The *New York Times*'s White House correspondent Elisabeth Bumiller became the poster child for deferential questioning when, at an academic forum, she responded to criticism about the press corps' passive behavior during President George W. Bush's prime-time news conference on the eve of the Iraq War by saying:

> *I think we were very deferential because ... it's live, it's very intense, it's frightening to stand up there. Think about it, you're standing up on prime-time live TV asking the president of the United States a question when the country's about to go to war. There was a very serious, somber tone that evening, and no one wanted to get into an argument with the president at this very serious time.*

Bumiller also went out of her way to defend the Bush Administration after Hurricane Katrina. When Bush was criticized for being photographed palling around with a musician on the day after the storm hit and the New Orleans levees failed, she wrote:

> *Bloggers... circulated a picture of Mr. Bush playing a guitar at an event in California on Tuesday to imply that he was fiddling while New Orleans drowned. In fact, the picture was taken when the country singer Mark Wills presented Mr. Bush with a guitar backstage at North Island Naval Air Station in Coronado, California, after Mr. Bush gave a speech marking the 60th anniversary of the Japanese surrender in World War II. Later that day, as floodwaters poured into New Orleans, Mr. Bush returned to his ranch in Texas, then left from his ranch for Washington on Wednesday morning.*

The *Times* story made it appear as if Bush promptly returned to Washington immediately after flooding began on Tuesday. But the levees failed on Monday, not Tuesday.

In the infamous case of Judith Miller, the problem was not a matter of deference but of outright complicity. She reported claims of active weapons programs fed to her by Iraqi exiles seeking Saddam Hussein's overthrow and "confirmed" by White House officials who were working directly with the exiles. The paper served the Administration's goal of building broad support for the war using dubious information.

Furthermore, after "major combat operations" ended, Miller inaccurately reported that a United States inspections team, with which she was embedded, found a site where weapons materials were buried. The *Times* eventually published an "Editor's Note" owning up to the faulty coverage, though the mea culpa was buried on page 10 and Miller was never admonished for it. (One-and-a-half years later, after her role in the CIA leak scandal surfaced, Miller negotiated a severance package and voluntarily left the paper.)

NPR, which has had its government funding threatened by Republicans ever since Democrats lost control of Congress in 1994, has also succumbed to right-wing pressure. When NPR listeners complained about the network's excessive use of conservative think tanks to provide analysis, its ombudsman responded in a December 2005 column that "NPR does not lean on the so-called conservative think tanks as many in the audience seem to think." His proof? In the past year NPR quoted conservative think tanks 239 times and liberal ones 141 times. The argument fully collapses once you realize that the "liberal" tanks cited by the ombudsman aren't actually liberal. They included only the Brookings Institution and the Center for Strategic and International Studies. Each houses experts from both parties and regularly churns out objective, rigorous research, not ideological missives. And in the case of CSIS, when one of your trustees is Henry Kissinger, that alone disqualifies you as liberal.

Another telling example of NPR's catering to conservatives was during the Supreme Court nomination hearings for John Roberts. NPR regularly discussed the nomination with two legal scholars, Jeffrey Rosen (a "liberal moderate" in his own words) and the conservative Doug Kmiec. Rosen, however, provided no balance. He joined Kmiec in continually praising Roberts.

As soon as the nomination was announced in July, Rosen said, "I am one of those many Democrats who will sing John Roberts's praises." In September he argued that while "there's every reason to believe he'll look a lot like Chief Justice Rehnquist," the conservative judge he was to replace, "he certainly won't move the court to the right and on some issues he might even move to the left." During the hearings, where many Democrats and liberals were frustrated at

Roberts's unwillingness to answer questions, Rosen extolled Roberts's performance, highlighting one response as "elegant." The segments left the false impression that no reasonable opposition to Roberts could exist.

Meanwhile, conservatives have succeeded in taking control of the Corporation for Public Broadcasting. As the *Washington Post* reported, "conservatives with close ties to the Bush administration have assumed control of every important position at the agency, which distributes about $400 million in federal funds to noncommercial radio and TV stations and is supposed to act as a buffer against outside political influence." That will only increase the right-wing pressure on the network.

INVADING THE ENEMY'S TURF

Engaging the conservative media is not as important as engaging the corporate media, since there's no way they will ever change how they do business. But that doesn't mean we shouldn't try. To undermine their arguments on their own turf can frustrate their ability to pressure the mainstream media. Also, note that a portion of every radio show's audience consists of moderates and liberals—one out of every four Rush Limbaugh listeners is not a self-described conservative—and their morale definitely could use some boosting.

Calling in to right-wing shows is not something to do lightly. If you can get past the screener, you'll be entering a rigged game. I've had the displeasure of calling into to Sean Hannity's program, so I know all too well that you not only will be shouted over, but your mic will be cut off at will, without your knowledge. You will think you have made strong points, but to the audience you'll sound disjointed and erratic. And you will never get the last word.

Fortunately, there's help in the blogosphere for those of you who still have a taste for mouth-to-mouth combat. Calling All Wingnuts (callingallwingnuts.com) offers tips on how to get through and conduct yourself on-air, tips such as "Get to know the host and identify their shtick" and "you never know when the host will cut you off, so . . . make your statement short." The blog drew blood in March 2006 when it organized readers to call Bill O'Reilly's radio show and praise MSNBC's Keith Olbermann. (Olbermann had been featuring O'Reilly in his daily "Worst Person in the World" segment whenever O'Reilly said anything particularly ridiculous, and O'Reilly had responded with an online petition for Olbermann's dismissal.)

After one guy managed to get through, O'Reilly abruptly disconnected the call at the mention of Olbermann's name, and threatened the caller on-air: "We have your phone number, and we're going to turn it over to Fox Security, and you'll be getting a little visit." He proceeded to threaten his entire audience, "When you call us, ladies and gentlemen . . . we do have your phone number." A man from "Fox News Security" then contacted a few pro-Olbermann callers, apparently to warn them they could be charged with harassment. Of course, that's nonsense. It's not harassment to call a call-in show just because the host doesn't agree with your opinion. The whole episode only served to give Olbermann more fodder and make O'Reilly look like he was losing his sanity. Calling All Wingnuts, 1; Conservatives, 0.

A MEGAPHONE, NOT A COCOON

Conservatives have declared war on every corner of the media and are successfully waging that war with their own media army. We must join the battle if we are ever to have a public-service media that allows American citizens to make well-informed decisions when charting the direction of their representative government.

With Air America and the liberal blogosphere, we are on our way to having the necessary ammo to win the war. These are not cocoons that separate us from the country. They are two-way communication mediums that allow us to share our own news analysis, freeing ourselves from dependence on shoddy corporate media for our comprehension of world events. They are activist assignment desks where we can both give and receive marching orders, so we both pressure the media to raise its standards, and defend the media from conservatives who want it permanently discredited. Ultimately, they create a megaphone that ensures that our voices are heard on *our* terms in the sprawling national conversation.

For the megaphone to work, it needs your voice.

STAY AND FIGHT

Engage the Corporate Media

✓When you read an article or hear a story, particularly in your local newspaper or on your local radio station, that does a good job of addressing an important issue, let the reporter and his or her editor know.

✓Regularly contact reporters and editors with ideas on how they can better inform their readers and function as a public service. Journalists are extremely busy, so always be brief. If you're writing a letter or e-mail, no more than 150 words.

✓ Encourage media to cover underreported stories and aggressively question political officials. Be polite—or be ignored.

✓ Every Friday or Saturday, suggest tough questions for Sunday talk show hosts to ask their guests. NBC's *Meet the Press*, ABC's *This Week* and CNN's *Late Edition* offer feedback forms on

their respective Web sites: http://www.msnbc.msn.com/
id/6872152/, http://abcnews.go.com/ThisWeek/story?id=
64596, and http://www.cnn.com/feedback/cnntv/. You can
contact CBS's *Face the Nation* via e-mail at ftn@cbsnews.com.

✓Use Air America Radio and the blogosphere as sources to track
conservative misinformation: check out Media Matters for
America (mediamatters.org), Fairness & Accuracy in Reporting (fair.org), and Newshounds (newshounds.us).

✓Join MoveOn.org's "Media Action" initiative, "to challenge
news outlets who abandon their journalistic duty to be a vigi-
lant watchdog for the public—asking tough questions to those
in power and getting to the bottom of stories." Sign up at civic.
moveon.org/mediaaction/join/.

CHAPTER 9

HOW TO BE A SAVVY PROTESTER

When you pray, move your feet.

—African proverb

What's the point of going to a protest rally? In the words of the National Organization for Women, from their *History of Marches and Mass Actions*, "Marches build and rejuvenate... by sending a message to those in power, and by forever changing the lives of participants."

I would qualify that a march *can* accomplish these things, if it 1) communicates a compelling message that resonates with the public, 2) moves citizens to take further action, and 3) achieves some tangible successes. There are plenty of poorly executed protests that fail to move public opinion, pressure political leaders, or attract new supporters, and therefore do not help energize the grassroots. For a true success story, look to the gold standard of protests, the 1963 March on Washington.

Sure, the march had a record turnout for its day (around a quarter of a million people) and was capped by a soaring speech by one of the finest orators in American history, Reverend Martin Luther King, Jr. But beyond "get a lot of people to show up" and "get great speakers," there are three other elements to a protest that citizens seeking to influence public opinion and the democratic process from the ground up should emulate.

1. COMMUNICATE A CLEAR MESSAGE

The March on Washington had a central focus: to pass the Civil Rights Act legislation proposed by President Kennedy.

Granted, the initial impetus of the march was far broader and loftier, as evidenced in the formal name, "March on Washington for Jobs and Freedom," and in the list of demands, which included a minimum wage hike, a public works program, and the end of school segregation. But once Kennedy introduced his bill, a few days after the march plans were announced, organizers wisely shifted their emphasis toward passing the bill.

In turn, great care was taken so that the speeches would collectively communicate the desired message. Most notably, when other march leaders found out at the last minute that one of the 10 scheduled speakers, John Lewis from the Student Nonviolent Coordinating Committee (SNCC), was planning to criticize the proposed Civil Rights Act as "too little, too late," they leaned on him to instead say, "We support it with great reservation," ensuring that he would not contradict the march's overall message.

2. PLAN CAREFULLY TO ENSURE GOOD TIMING

In the case of the March on Washington, the good timing was more by luck than by design, as the Civil Rights Act was introduced after the march was conceived. But having a concrete proposal on the table gave the march the opportunity to achieve a tangible success, because a strong public push could influence wavering, hesitant lawmakers. Holding a march that was not timed to influence any specific action, just to prove the organizers could generate a large crowd, would not have yielded results. The energy created by such a rally would not have had been channeled in a constructive way.

3. THINK THROUGH YOUR PRESENTATION

By coming together in large numbers and attracting media attention, protesters send a visual message to millions of Americans watching at home. Making a positive impression is essential to expanding the base of support.

For example, David C. Ruffin recounted his March on Washington experience in *Focus*, the magazine of the Joint Center for Political and Economic Studies, and talked about the importance participants put on their outward appearance:

> *Many of the men wore coats and ties; the women wore print dresses. Their attire seemed impractical for a march and day long rally in Washington's summer heat and humidity, but the people on this train were on their way to conduct serious business. They were presenting themselves at the seat of their government to seek redress for more than 300 years of racism and injustice.*

In fact, such a premium was placed on image that SNCC leader Stokely Carmichael complained afterward that the march amounted to "a sanitized, middle-class version of the real black movement." Whether or not that was a fair criticism, the reality is that the march worked.

Polls before (and after) the march showed a discomfort, among whites, with mass demonstrations for civil rights. Any image that played into that discomfort might have sparked a major backlash and slowed the movement's progress. The march organizers avoided that pitfall. Presenting an image of "serious business" helped garner much favorable media coverage (as did a extremely well-executed media relations effort, including a large "News HQ" tent and more than 1,600 special press passes).

APPLYING THE LESSONS IN LOS ANGELES

Because so many protests in recent years have failed to spark lasting change, the March on Washington can seem like a moment in history never to be duplicated. But the March 2006 immigrant rights rally that attracted a half million Los Angelenos, and the immigration-related protests across the country that followed, proved that notion wrong.

The protesters had a clear message: Stop the House bill that would turn working immigrants into felons and put a 700-mile wall on the Mexican border. The timing was perfect. The Senate was considering its own legislation in response to the House, and the strong turnout was a warning shot to Republican politicians worried about their ability to attract Latino votes. And the presentation was thought through, as organizers successfully urged participants to wear white shirts to symbolize peace and to carry American flags to show their love of their adopted country.

Thanks to flawless execution, the protesters saw real results right away. Two days later, the Senate Judiciary Committee approved a bill that rejected the House approach and created a path to citizenship for those working in America illegally.

MESSAGELESS IN SEATTLE

After the November 1999 protests against the World Trade Organization meeting in Seattle, organizers were hopeful that the anti-globalization movement would continue to grow, especially since they were able to bring together a wide array of groups, including environmentalists, unions, and self-described anarchists. But the horrible presentation detracted from their core message about fair global trade.

Forget about the property destruction of store windows, which was the fault of only a few. (One prominent Seattle anarchist publicly lashed out at a small group of Eugene, Oregon, anarchists for violating a nonviolence agreement.) More important, the images of the peaceful marches did not show a diverse coalition unifying around a clear message but a motley crew with a cacophony of messages. As *Boston Phoenix* reporter Jason Gay observed, it was a protest for those who "had a beef about anything from trade tariffs to netted sea turtles to Starbucks."

Many Americans who are concerned about poorly designed trade agreements did not see a place for themselves in the chaos and did not sign up for the movement. Subsequent protests of international meetings on U.S. soil have declined in size and have not affected our trade policy.

SIZE DOESN'T MATTER
AS MUCH AS YOU THINK

The April 2004 March for Women's Lives, held on the Mall in Washington, was twice the size of the immigrant rights rally, and it may well have been the biggest protest rally in American history. Yet it left no mark on society. Today, few outside the women's rights community could even tell you that it happened.

Neither the message nor the timing was pegged to pass or stop any pending government proposal, policy, or appointment. The march slogan, "Choice—Justice—Access—Health—Abortion—Global Family Planning," was too general in its support for all aspects of reproductive rights. No singular message was offered in the more than 100 speeches. (The March on Washington, had a relatively compact speakers' list of 10, which better controlled the march's message.) Speakers drifted into various tangential issues such as the separation of church and state and the curtailing of civil liberties after 9/11.

Most media coverage simply said that the march was about supporting abortion rights. That's a simple yet vague message, as it doesn't tell the public what needs to be done to protect those rights, let alone why those rights are important. In the end they had a one-day show of support but without a call and a plan for concrete action that could channel the grassroots energy after the day was over.

Some march supporters argued afterward that the event didn't have a major impact because it didn't get the media coverage it deserved, citing a report from Fairness and Accuracy in Reporting which found that recent marches of lesser size received more coverage. The fallacy is that a big crowd automatically warrants lots of news coverage. Without a clear message, there's just not as much news to report.

SOMETIMES, ONE PERSON IS ENOUGH

In contrast, take Cindy Sheehan's protest outside of President George W. Bush's Crawford, Texas, ranch in August 2005. It was designed as a protest of one: a mom who lost her son in the Iraq War, taking on Bush during his annual month-long vacation.

Sheehan had a clear message, a single question: "What was the noble cause my son died in?" That's the classic hardball question disguised as a softball. It should have been a no-brainer to explain the "noble cause" to her and the public 2 years after the war began. But Bush hadn't been able to sufficiently explain it ever since the failure to find weapons of mass destruction in Iraq. Sheehan's question further exposed the inability of the White House to provide a firm rationale for war and contributed to the war's declining public support in 2005.

Sheehan also had good timing. Her protest took place while Bush was on an extended vacation at a time when U.S. casualties were mounting, making him appear out of touch and putting him on the defensive. And she did so during a month that news editors consider to be a slow news month, when they are especially hungry for stories. She had good presentation, too, credibly portraying herself as an "everymom," channeling the concerns that many military parents were having about the protracted conflict. She even inspired other mothers to travel to Crawford and join the protest, generating additional news coverage.

However, Sheehan diminished her impact soon after the August protest with her next move: intentionally getting arrested in front of the White House with other protesters. This was poor timing and poor presentation. Sheehan had just successfully defined herself as an everymom. But your average mother doesn't get herself arrested.

Certainly there are times when peaceful civil disobedience is a smart, even dignified, tactic, and there are times when a high-profile arrest can force the media to cover an issue that otherwise would be ignored. But Sheehan had no need to resort to such measures right after achieving such stature and prominence. For her, being photographed in the arms of police officers was a step backward, downgrading her everymom image, with which many Americans had identified, to a one of a stereotypical protester, to which fewer Americans related. Instead, Sheehan should have stayed true to her persona and her message. She could have led a group of military mothers in following Bush around the country and pressuring him to answer the "noble cause" question. Including only mothers would have kept the size of the protests down, but as with her solo protest, it would have provided a powerful visual image and helped articulate a consistent, substantive message.

GROWING YOUR NEIGHBORHOOD GRASSROOTS

Okay, so you want to organize a protest but you're not the head of an organization with thousands of members. How can you, a mere citizen, unleash the people power of your community? First, you have to connect with others.

The Internet is making that easier. Howard Dean was able to build a volunteer network of disaffected Democrats through Meetup.com, a site that allows people to find clubs in the area or create their own which helped propel his dark-horse 2004 presidential campaign to frontrunner status. Los Angeles high school students organized a 15,000-person walkout in support of immigrant rights by spreading the word within the sprawling online community www.myspace.com. DrinkingLiberally.org, an informal club with more than 130 chapters in watering holes across the country, is not only a fun way to meet folks with whom to talk politics; it also encourages local activism, from organizing phone banks to becoming Democratic precinct captains.

If you're regularly bonding with like-minded neighbors, either around a particular issue or around liberalism generally, when the timing is right for a citizen action in the streets you'll have the means to make it happen. When your neighbors see how successful you were, they'll be more inclined to join your network.

What will it take for your local protest to be perceived as successful?

Keep in mind that outside of big cities you don't need tens of thousands of people to make a splash in the local media. A rally of a few hundred is often enough to grab attention and get a single message out.

You want that message to make a lasting impact in your community, so stick to issues that directly affect your community, at least initially. You may get a few hundred people to turn out for an antiwar rally, but your town council didn't start a war and doesn't have the means to stop it. You'll have a better shot of achieving tangible progress if you focus on things like raising your state or local minimum wage, expanding health care coverage, improving services for the poor, protecting your area schools from corporate or fringe fundamentalist influence, preventing detrimental commercial development, or supporting environmentally safe and economically sound development.

Once you score some local victories and feed the strength of your community network, you'll be poised to do your part when the time is right for a nationwide protest.

CONSERVATIVES PROTEST TOO

It's particularly imperative for liberals to get better at protesting because conservatives are making strides, if the success of "Justice Sunday" in April 2005 is any indication.

Justice Sunday—sponsored by the Family Research Council, which in its own words "promotes the Judeo-Christian worldview as the basis for a just, free, and stable society"—was a relatively small rally of only a few thousand in a Louisville, Kentucky, church. However, it was aired on Christian TV and on a Web site, expanding the event's reach.

(Organizers sought to inflate the size of the TV audience by saying the program "reached 61 million households." That is a meaningless figure, as the number of households the program "reached" is not the number of households that actually "watched" but the number of households that had access to the telecast. If anything, that number speaks to the limited reach of the channels that aired it, as there are about 110 million TV households in the country. If 61 million households really did watch, it would mean more people watched Justice Sunday than the *Seinfeld* finale. Didn't happen.)

The rally had a clear message—"Stop the Filibuster Against People of Faith"—which succinctly, albeit dishonestly, argued that Senate Democrats were blocking judicial nominees because the nominees believed in God. The message was helped along by the event's provocative poster, featuring a boy holding a gavel in one hand and a Bible in the other, under the tagline, "He Should Not Have to Choose." And Justice Sunday was timed well, during a suspenseful showdown over a handful of right-wing nominees for the federal appeals courts (the level directly below the Supreme Court). Speakers drilled the audience to contact specific senators and urge them to support the nominees, giving participants a way to channel the energy that the event created toward a productive purpose.

The media coverage and calls to Congress had a positive effect—from a right-wing perspective. While Democrats had not lost any confirmation battles over right-wing court nominees during President George W. Bush's first term, soon after Justice Sunday, enough

Democrats cracked under the pressure to allow most of the controversial nominees to get confirmed.

Granted, Justice Sunday was merely one successful protest. But it should be a wake-up call for liberals and Democrats alike. If conservatives are able to regularly execute successful citizen actions and we are not, then it's the conservative movement and the Republicans, fairly or unfairly, that will be perceived as being fueled by "people power" and representing the grassroots.

To prevent that outcome, we don't necessarily need more protests or bigger protests. We just need savvier protests.

STAY AND FIGHT

How to Be a Savvy Protester

✓For the basics on putting together a rally of your own, check out 51 Capital March's protest logistics checklist at 51capital-march.com.

✓Aim for tangible success by focusing on issues affecting your local or regional community.

✓No need to think big. Outside of major cities, a well-executed protest of moderate size is likely to make an impact and help grow your group for future action.

✓ Keep your event focused around a simple, straightforward message. Don't push an assortment of random causes. Encourage participants to stay on-point in their speeches, signs, literature, and comments to the press.

✓ TV, radio, and newspaper journalists can't report on your event unless they know about it in advance. Find out which local reporters cover the issues at hand. Fax or e-mail a media advisory that includes the "who, what, when, where, and why" of your protest. Follow up with a phone call to make sure it was received and to see whether the reporter has any questions. Don't badger. If you've done things right, they will come.

✓Encourage fellow protesters to dress for success. You will make a better impression on those who catch a glimpse of a rally on TV or in a newspaper if you look like you're conducting serious business.

✓Contact relevant elected officials the next day and help translate the rally's energy into concrete action.

✓Set up tables with voter registration forms at rallies, so we can maximize our numbers on Election Day.

CHAPTER 10

GET ON THE 'NET, GET OUT OF THE HOUSE, GET A LIBERAL AMERICA

At this point in the book, you're undoubtedly feeling so inspired to fight for your liberal principles and rights that you're no longer even remotely tempted to move to Canada by the siren song of Celine Dion or the savory scent of poutine. Or, perhaps you read that Canada elected a Conservative prime minister in January 2006 and you realize that turning tail and quitting America is ultimately futile. Either way, you're here to stay.

So, what should you do once you put this book down? How best should you invest your energy, time, and disposable income to help achieve our ideal version of America? How can we work together to maximize our influence?

For too long we have been at the mercy of what has been called the Republican Noise Machine or the Mighty Wurlitzer—that network of right-wing philanthropic foundations, think tanks, theocratic organizations, media outlets, and pundits which deftly swamps our political discourse with lies and smears dressed up as journalism and scholarship. Our individual voices have been no match for this well-coordinated apparatus. But that's beginning to change. An infrastructure of our own is being built up so that we can define ourselves and prevent the spread of misinformation. Let's call it the Liberal Truth Machine.

The Center for American Progress and the Institute for America's Future are think tanks with sibling organizations—American Progress Action Fund and Campaign for America's Future, respectively—that translate ideas into action. The Progressive Legislative Action Network develops and advocates policy ideas for all 50 state legislatures. MoveOn.org, boasting more than 3 million members, mobilizes the grassroots via the Internet around a broad range of issues. Democracy for America, created by Howard Dean after his failed presidential bid and now run by his brother, Jim, recruits and trains "fiscally responsible, socially progressive" candidates for public office. Wellstone Action, founded by the children of the late liberal icon Senator Paul Wellstone, teaches community organizing and voter mobilization skills. Christian Alliance for Progress, CrossLeft, founded in 2005, and Tikkun's Network for Spiritual Progressives, all are beginning to organize religious liberals.

Air America Radio and the liberal blogosphere gives all this energy and activity the megaphone necessary to affect national discourse. Media Matters for America plays a defensive role, continually debunking the misinformation that right-wing operatives try to inject into the media bloodstream, and an offensive role, putting pressure on media outlets to resist such misinformation.

If the pieces are falling into the place, does that mean that we can just sit back and watch the Liberal Truth Machine pound the Mighty Wurlitzer until it can barely spit out "Chopsticks"? Absolutely not. Our machine won't be fully assembled, and it won't function as effectively as possible, until we all play an active role.

JOIN THE LIBERAL TRUTH MACHINE

People can be too quick to trumpet the power of the Internet, as if it's a magical force that automatically makes everything better. It's not. It's a tool. It can be used well or used poorly.

One person who has been in the business of using it well is Peter Daou, a political consultant who specializes in online communications. He directed "online rapid response and blog outreach" for John Kerry's presidential campaign, and he now produces *The Daou Report*, Salon.com's 24-7 roundup of online political commentary.

In an interview, Daou told me that "the Internet should be the central organizing tool" in building a 21st century liberal infrastructure because "it's merely the fastest way, and the most direct and honest way, to share information . . . the quickest way to fact-check, to move stuff around, to develop . . . message[s], and to learn."

For the Internet to be an effective tool, the liberal blogosphere needs a critical mass of individuals. Daou counsels people that Internet participation is the most important thing one can do.

> *Join [a] blog or online community. Talk online and become part of this network, because the bigger this network grows, the more influence it will have. . . . When you have 2 million people online, it can be very different from when you have 10 million people online, all talking and chatting [and] put[ing] pressure on representatives and [the] media.*

So, if you're not already part of the blogosphere, how do you join?

The popularity of blogs partly stems from how easy it is start one. You can set up a blog for free at Blogger.com or WordPress.com, while SixApart.com offers blogging services that can cost about $50 per year. Within seconds, you can publicly share ideas, information, and analysis with the rest of the blogosphere. The tricky part, however, is not in the starting but in the sharing.

As the blogosphere grows, it becomes harder for new entrants to call attention to themselves, which can lead to frustration and very short blogging tenures. The blogosphere works best when bloggers spread information widely and keep traffic flowing by regularly linking to each others' posts. But the top bloggers, who now attract tens if not hundreds of thousands of daily readers, are swamped with link requests and can't possibly accommodate everyone.

Therefore, the best way for new bloggers to hook up with the rest of the blogosphere is to e-mail a few blogs with moderate-size audiences, and moderately full inboxes, when you have posted novel, useful commentary that would be of interest that those particular bloggers (as opposed to "blast e-mailing" every single post you do to a enormous list of bloggers, which is a sure way to get your e-mail deleted, if not getting your e-mail address permanently blocked by those recipients).

If engaging in self-promotion isn't your style, you're better off not starting your own blog. Instead, participate in existing blogosphere communities—huge yet independently run sites such as dailykos.com, atrios.blogspot.com, and tpmcafe.com; official Democratic Party blogs such as the Democratic National Committee's democrats.org/blog, the House Democrats' blog.dccc.org, and the Senate Democrats' fromtheroots.org; blogs that arm you with information and analysis not found in traditional media, such as juancole.com, digbysblog.blogspot.com, and my own LiberalOasis.com; and blogs with a state or local focus, such as Illinois' archpundit.com, Texas' burntorangereport.com, and Montana's leftinthewest.com.

How does one participate in these communities? Most blogs include links where readers can tack their own thoughts directly onto the blogger's original post, sparking dialogue with other readers as well as the lead bloggers. Tips from readers are often picked up by the lead bloggers and used for posts on the main page, allowing readers the ability to have their ideas spread throughout the blogosphere.

FUND THE LIBERAL TRUTH MACHINE

One reason the Noise Machine has been so influential is that its donors support efforts to articulate a broad vision of conservatism, whereas liberal and left-leaning funders typically have backed small-bore projects.

The liberal think tank Commonweal Institute, in its January 2005 report, *Creating Progressive Infrastructure Now*, cited a finding by the National Committee for Responsive Philanthropy: "Conservative foundations have, in part, been so effective not so much due to the size of their grants but rather because they tend to give more to general operating support." Commonweal then concluded:

> *The traditional foundation funding model, which uses narrow guidelines and proposals, is slower and more cumbersome, and seldom provides the unrestricted funds needed for major institutional growth. This model is valuable for funding specific projects, but, as currently structured, it is not appropriate for building a substantial, flexible, and interlinked [progressive infrastructure] rapidly.*

Commonweal's critique was targeted at well-heeled foundations, but parallel logic applies to the legion of current and potential individual small donors. People are often inclined to give to a specific cause dear to them—saving a species, protecting civil liberties, providing access to abortion—because it's easy to visualize where your money is going and what it is doing. Organizations fighting for those causes are by no means flush with cash. They still need our financial support. But putting money into think tanks, media outlets, blogs, and community-based activist organizations to build up the "general operating support" of a liberal movement is an urgent priority.

So we don't cannibalize ourselves by feeding the new and starving the old, we need additional financial resources. Since most of us aren't trust fund babies, the way to do that is enlarging the pool of individual small donors. As the community of liberals who join the Truth Machine and participate online grows, so will that pool.

COORDINATE THE LIBERAL TRUTH MACHINE

If the community of liberals who actively participate in the new liberal infrastructure grows, and in turn small-donor funding of the infrastructure grows, it won't mean much unless all that grassroots energy is productively channeled. That can't happen without good leadership.

However, movements typically do not have singular leaders. For instance, Dr. Martin Luther King, Jr., was not the lone leader of the civil rights movement. He headed up one organization of that movement, the Southern Christian Leadership Conference, which coordinated with the NAACP, the Urban League, and others. Today's conservative movement is not singularly led either. It holds a weekly session known as the "Wednesday Meeting" so that fringe fundamentalist and crony corporate factions can coordinate with each other.

Achieving an effective level of coordination is not the primary responsibility of the grassroots members of the Liberal Truth Machine but of those who lead the infrastructure's various organizations. If those leaders lack the requisite people skills and checked egos, they won't work well together and the machine's cogs won't be in sync.

Nevertheless, the grassroots can play a role. As Daou notes, the blogosphere gives individuals a medium to "put pressure on representatives." "Pressure" does not always take the form of brute force; it can also be applied with constructive criticism. And "representatives" does not only mean your elected representatives. Organizations that are spearheading the liberal movement are indirectly representing you when they campaign for goals that you support.

They need to hear from us. They need to hear from people with an outsiders' perspective who can spot things that myopic insiders miss. They need to hear it when they're doing stuff right so they'll keep doing it, and when they're doing stuff wrong so they'll get better.

So, when you notice liberal leaders failing to communicate uniform messages on a particular issue, or focusing on separate issues when they should be joining forces on a pressing issue, point it out to them. Nudge them to get on the same page. Constantly remind them that unless we're coordinated at the top, we will not be able to articulate a compelling vision of a liberal America—and conversely, an unappealing vision of a conservative America—and have it be clearly heard throughout today's cluttered and manipulated media landscape.

GET OUT OF THE HOUSE

In the end, we can win back America only on Election Day. If all of the energy spent talking, chatting, calling, writing, blogging, and e-mailing from the comfort of our homes doesn't translate into energy on the sidewalks and at the polls, then all our fancy new tools are as useful as a robot dog.

That means you can't always be in front of a computer. You have get out and engage your friends and neighbors. As Christopher Hayes of *In These Times* reported in "How to Turn Your Red State Blue," "face-to-face canvassing is far and away the most effective means of persuasion: Roughly 1 out of every 15 voters approached at the door will add their vote to your tally."

How can the Internet help get more people to knock on doors? Look at what Howard Dean did when became chairman of the Democratic National Committee (DNC). He created a "Neighbor-to-Neighbor National Organizing Day" on April 29, 2006. He announced it a month ahead of time on the party's official blog and others, and in an e-mail to supporters. The announcements linked to a web page where people could find events in their zip code or create their own; download doorhangers, flyers, and scripts; and get canvassing tips. Without spending much money on advertising, the party was able to deliver marching orders across the country in seconds, channeling the efforts of the grassroots.

The Internet can not only help the Democratic Party reach out to potential supporters, it can also help us reform the party from the inside. Take the example of Jenny Greenleaf, a self-described "progressive" who proclaimed on the American Street blog in 2004 that "the Party needs to regain its soul as well as its backbone." Instead of simply complaining about it, she got elected to serve as a DNC member from Oregon, defeating a 16-year veteran committee-woman in part by whipping up support in the blogosphere. She continues to communicate with the grassroots via several blogs, including westerndemocrat.com, mydd.com, and the official DNC blog, where she wrote, "I'm a poster child for the ease of taking over the Party. You can do it too. Go sign up."

TENACITY AND FAITH: KEYS TO ULTIMATE VICTORY

The conservative movement has enough conviction to proudly state its core principles but not enough faith in the public to submit those principles to open and honest debate. That's why it operates as a Noise Machine designed to buffet those principles on a bed of lies and distortions. Up until now, liberal activists and Democratic Party leaders have not consistently articulated a set of core principles, nor have they found a way to combat conservative misinformation, and so the Noise Machine has held the edge.

But the Liberal Truth Machine is now poised to gain the upper hand because of its faith in *you*. You, and all other Americans, have a renewed ability to shape liberal principles in both domestic and foreign policy. If we, as members of the Liberal Truth Machine, can proudly and thoughtfully articulate our liberal principles, the faith will eventually run both ways—Americans will hold the same trust in liberalism that liberalism holds in Americans. Only then will a liberal America be realized.

Such idealism must be sharpened with a realistic approach to corporate media and a bottomless appetite for debunking right-wing falsehoods before they spread. At the same time, we cannot allow the need for constant fact-checking to keep us perpetually on the defensive, giving the Mighty Wurlitzer the power to dictate the debate. While beating back misinformation, we must also proactively seek opportunities to showcase the value of liberal principles. For a Liberal Truth Machine to accomplish so much requires ample resources: vision, money, and bodies.

And there's one other thing we will need: tenacity, if for no other reason than our opponent has it in spades. These guys lost the battle over birth control and abortion at the highest court in the land, in 1965 and 1973, respectively, and they have never stopped fighting to deny both. They lost the battle over progressive taxation in 1913 with the passage of the Sixteenth Amendment of the U.S. Constitution, but that didn't deter them from pushing for multimillionaires to pay the same tax rates as those who live paycheck to paycheck. They lost yet another battle over Social Security in 2005, and you can bet they will come back, again and again, to try to dismantle the promise of a secure retirement.

The persistence of the conservative movement is why the strategies that make up this book are not quick-fix solutions. They are guidelines for seizing and maintaining the upper hand in a protracted struggle with no definitive end. I have attempted to define liberal principles succinctly, but they are not magic buzzwords that will permanently change minds by their mere utterance. They are principles that, when consistently used to frame and support specific policy positions, will build trust over time.

And don't expect leading Washington Democrats to lead the effort to reclaim the label "liberal." They are hardwired to focus on the election in front of them, which makes them apprehensive of any strategy that doesn't pay off right away. Fortunately, the Democratic Party is not owned by a few people at the top. Power in the party is increasingly decentralized. Volunteers and small-money donors are having more influence on the direction of the party than ever before.

If we take the lead on the airwaves, in our communities, on the letters-to-the-editor page, and on the blogs, reassociating "liberal" with the values and beliefs that speak to Americans' struggles and desires in an insecure economy and destabilized world, we will reform the Democratic Party, giving it the strength and savvy to regain the trust of the voting public.

As with any protracted struggle, the effort to revitalize liberalism will include ups and downs, frustrations, lessons learned, and adjustments. There will be episodes of confidence, doubt, hope, cynicism, jubilation, and exhaustion. There will be hard losses to shake off, fleeting victories to look past, and real victories to build on.

The conservative movement, lacking faith in their ideas and the public, desperately hopes that we will be worn down by the struggle and eventually stop fighting. As Grover Norquist wishfully mused following the Democratic defeat in the 2004 elections:

> *Once the minority of House and Senate are comfortable in their minority status, they will have no problem socializing with the Republicans. Any farmer will tell you that certain animals run around and are unpleasant, but when they've been fixed, then they are happy and sedate. They are contented and cheerful. They don't go around peeing on the furniture and such.*

That is the choice before us? To basically become neutered farm animals? To passively allow the conservative movement to take away our government and put it in the hands of crony corporate executives and fringe fundamentalist leaders?

Wouldn't you rather stay and fight: for a representative, responsive, responsible government; for fair and adequate taxation; for fostering democracy and prosperity, not destruction and hypocrisy, across the globe; for real religious liberty; for a media that serves the public; for a judiciary that upholds the Constitution for all, not perverts it at the behest of a few?

With bedrock principles to steady us, and with a strong infrastructure fueled by millions of passionate and patriotic Americans, we can withstand the setbacks, overcome the lies, earn political clout, and keep up the fight until America once again has, in the words of political survivor Jimmy Carter, a government as good as its people.

STILL NOT CONVINCED?

I had hoped it wouldn't come to this. I wanted to stay positive and upbeat. But if you're still harboring fantasies of moving to Canada, I have no choice but to tell you the hard truth about life up north.

- Global warming will take out Canada first.
- *Wildest Royal Canadian Mounted Police Chase Videos* doesn't hold a candle to *Cops*.
- America's #1 export to Canada? Pollution.
- There. Is. No. BBQ.
- The "War on Boxing Day" has gotten way out of hand.
- The curling in Minnesota is superior. That's right. I said it.
- Thrill-seekers never experience the adrenaline rush of going without health insurance.
- There is such a thing as too much Barenaked Ladies.
- An angry pack of beavers is not a pretty sight.
- If we cede America to Republicans, they'll eventually invade Canada anyway.

ACKNOWLEDGMENTS

Thanks to everyone who helped make this book possible and contributed in ways large and small: My editors Leigh Haber and Chris Potash of Rodale, my agents Danielle Svetcov and Daniel Greenberg of Levine Greenberg, Lorraine Sciarra, Stephen Sherrill, Josh Orton, Rev. Dr. Peter Ives, Frederick Clarkson, Pastor Elise Brown, Rev. Tim Simpson, Ashley Weinard, "Alonzo," Eban Polk, Christy Polk, Sarah Johnson, Mark Hayes, Katie Reeder-Hayes, Andrew Rowell, Mary Mathew, Maureen McFadden, Leslie Calman, Jane Gruenebaum, Jessica Valenti, Joey Fishkin, Stacey Mink, David McCormick, David Linker, James Kim, Jason Keadjian, Donna Riley, John Halpin and Center for American Progress, David Grossman and Media Matters for America, and of course, all the readers and supporters of LiberalOasis.com.

SOURCES

Introduction

Senator Bob Dole's remarks come from a November 4, 1992, press conference transcribed by the Federal News Service.

House Minority Leader Nancy Pelosi's remarks were made in the November 6, 2004, weekly Democratic Radio Address.

Then-Senator-elect Barack Obama's remarks were made on NBC's *Meet the Press* on November 7, 2004.

Air America Radio listenership statistics come from then-CEO Danny Goldberg's 9/28/05 blog post on The Huffington Post titled "Right Wing Media Gets Desperate," www.huffingtonpost.com/danny-goldberg/right-wing-media-gets-des_b_8029.html.

Chapter 1

Senator Lindsey Graham's quote was made on the 7/11/04 edition of ABC's *This Week with George Stephanopoulos*.

Harris Poll data come from the 1/18/06 report titled "Harris Polls throughout 2005 Suggest Modest Gain by Democrats in Party Affiliation."

Poll showing support for government responsibility on health care and poverty comes from a Greenberg Quinlan Rosner Research, Inc., 11/12/03 memorandum titled "Taxes, Government and the Obligations of Citizenship."

Poll showing support for infrastructure spending over tax cuts done by the *Los Angeles Times* between January 15 and 17, 2005. Data available at www.pollingreport.com/budget.htm.

Poll on gays in the military done by *USA Today*/CNN/Gallup from November 19 to 21, 2004. Data available at www.usatoday.com/news/polls/tables/live/2004-11-22-poll.htm.

Poll data showing support for gay marriage or civil unions come from the 2004 presidential election voter exit poll. Data available at www.cnn.com/ELECTION/2004/pages/results/states/US/P/00/epolls.0.html.

Poll data about Supreme Court justices and Roe come from *Washington Post*–ABC surveys taken during the John Roberts and Sam Alito nominations. Data available at www.washingtonpost.com/wp-dyn/content/custom/2005/12/20/CU2005122001059.html.

John F. Kennedy's nomination acceptance speech to the New York Liberal Party is available at www.pbs.org/wgbh/amex/presidents/35_kennedy/psources/ps_nyliberal.html.

Information on Richard Nixon's approval ratings comes from the article "Bill Clinton, CEO" in the April 1998 copy of the *Wall Street Journal*, Classroom Edition.

Background on Jimmy Carter's ad campaign against Ted Kennedy comes from "The Pursuit of the Presidency 1980" by David Broder, Lou Cannon, Haynes Johnson, Martin Schram, Richard Harwood and the staff of *The Washington Post*.

The New York Times's characterization of the 1984 Democratic convention appeared in the 7/22/84 article, "Democrats' Platform Shows a Shift from Liberal Positions of 1976 and 1980." Further background available in the September 1992 *Extra!* magazine article, "Conventional Wisdom: How the Press Rewrites Democratic Party History Every Four Years."

Transcripts of presidential nomination acceptance speeches can be found at www.4president.org. Transcripts of presidential debates can be found at www.debates.org.

The exchange between Michael Dukakis and ABC News's Ted Koppel was published in *Pledging Allegiance*, by Sidney Blumenthal.

1988 Gallup tracking poll data was published in "The Quest for the Presidency 1988" by Peter Goldman, Tom Mathews and the *Newsweek* Special Election Team.

Chapter 2

Stan and Anna Greenberg poll data come from a Greenberg Quinlan Rosner Research, Inc., 11/12/03 memorandum titled "Taxes, Government and the Obligations of Citizenship."

George W. Bush's remarks on Social Security were made on April 18, 2005, at the South Carolina Statehouse. Full transcript available at www.whitehouse.gov/news/releases/2005/04/20050418-1.html.

The version of the Sen. John Breaux Medicare story quoted here comes from his Senate floor statement of October 3, 1996, which can be found at http://thomas.loc.gov.

The characterization of the conservative strategy memo regarding Bill Clinton's health care plans came from the document "A Detailed Timeline of the Healthcare Debate portrayed in *The System*," posted on the Web site for the PBS program, *The NewsHour with Jim Lehrer*. *The System* is a book by David Broder and Haynes Johnson about Clinton's failure to pass health care reform. The PBS timeline is available at www.pbs.org/newshour/forum/may96/background/health_debate_page2.html.

Newt Gingrich's remarks before Bill Clinton's 1994 State of the Union Address were made January 25, 1994, on CNN during an interview conducted by Judy Woodruff.

For more about the failings of the No Child Left Behind law, see the 2/24/05 article "Legislators Demand Change in No Child Left Behind Law" from Stateline.org, and the 10/21/04 article "The Issue Left Behind" by Linda Perlstein in the online edition of *The Nation*.

For details about the Bush Administration's record on toxic waste cleanup, see the 10/29/04 article "Paying Double for Pollution" by the Sierra Club's Ed Hopkins, published by TomPaine.com.

See how poverty has risen during the Bush presidency by going to the poverty section of the Census.gov Web site, www.census.gov/hhes/www/poverty/poverty.html.

Chapter 3

Information about the tax filing process comes from a speech by House Democratic Whip Steny Hoyer, delivered 7/13/04 at the Tax Policy Center Forum, available at www.democraticwhip.house.gov/media/statements.cfm?pressReleaseID=775.

The National Public Radio segment on Grover Norquist ran on the 5/25/01 *Morning Edition*. For more about the conservative "Starve the Beast" strategy, see "The Tax-Cut Con" by Paul Krugman in the 9/14/03 edition of *The New York Times Magazine*, and "Starving The Beast" by Ed Kilgore in the 6/30/03 edition of *Blueprint* magazine.

Information on the public reaction to Walter Mondale's nominating convention came from "A Running Start" in the 7/30/84 edition of *Newsweek* and the 7/31/84 Associated Press article "Harris: Mondale Within Two Points of Reagan."

Information on Ronald Reagan's uneven response to Mondale on tax increases can be found in the 8/8/84 *New York Times* article, "Reagan on the Defensive" by Steven Weisman, and the 8/4/84 *National Journal* article, "Mondale's Gamble On Tax Increase Could Pay Off If Fairness Becomes the Issue" by William Schneider.

Economic data for 1996 are from the "Issues '96" webpage co-sponsored by *The New York Times* and National Public Radio, available at www.nytimes.com/specials/issues/money/monhome/synop.html.

Bill Clinton's quote from October 1995 about his tax increase comes from a transcript of his remarks available at www.clintonfoundation.org/legacy/101795-speech-by-president-at-president-gala-dinner.htm.

Bill Clinton's characterizations of competing tax cut plans were made in the 10/6/96 presidential debate; transcript available at www.debates.org/pages/trans96a.html. George W. Bush's remarks were made in the 10/3/00 debate; transcript available at www.debates.org/pages/trans2000a.html.

Poll showing support for infrastructure spending over tax cuts done by the *Los Angeles Times* between January 15 and 17, 2005, and also between December 12 and 15, 2002. Associated Press–Ipsos poll regarding tax cuts and balanced budgets was conducted between November 3 and 5, 2004. Data available at www.pollingreport.com/budget.htm.

Background on Pell Grants is from the 12/23/04 *New York Times* article, "Students to Bear More of the Cost of College" and the 10/18/04 CNN/*Money* article, "College Costs Spike Again," available at money.cnn.com/2004/10/18/pf/college/college_costs.

Data on job training cuts are available at the AFL-CIO analysis of the Bush Administration's 2007 budget, at www.aflcio.org/issues/bushwatch/2007budget.cfm.

Information on Veterans Administration spending comes from the March 2005 Congressional Budget Office report "The Potential Cost of Meeting Demand for Veterans' Health Care," the 6/24/05 *Washington Post* article "Funds for Health Care of Veterans $1 Billion Short," and the 3/16/06 Democratic Policy Committee document "A Look at the Fuzzy Math Behind the Administration's Proposed Increase in Veterans Health Spending."

Information on science labs moving overseas comes from ABCNews.com columnist Lee Dye's 12/2/04 piece, "U.S. Falling Behind in Science," available at abcnews.go.com/Technology/print?id=276464, and from the 4/14/05 article "Pulling the Plug on Science?" by Peter N. Spotts of the *Christian Science Monitor*.

Bill Clinton's attacks on Paul Tsongas were reported by *The Boston Globe*'s Adam Pertman and Martin F. Nolan on 2/28/92 in the piece, "Democratic Vitriol Spreads As Clinton Rips Tsongas."

Chapter 4

Gary Hart quote is from a 10/7/04 interview by the online magazine The Globalist, available at www.theglobalist.com/DBWeb/StoryId.aspx?StoryId=4164.

Paul Freedman's election analysis in Slate, "The Gay Marriage Myth," is available at www.slate.com/id/2109275.

Poll data regarding 2004 voter views on Iraq come from the 2004 presidential election voter exit poll. Data available at www.cnn.com/ELECTION/2004/pages/results/states/US/P/00/epolls.0.html.

George W. Bush's 2005 inaugural address is available at www.whitehouse.gov/news/releases/2005/01/20050120-1.html. His prior remarks regarding past Western policy toward Middle East dictators were made on 11/6/03 and are available at www.whitehouse.gov/news/releases/2003/11/20031106-2.html.

Information on the human rights record of Pakistan comes from Human Rights Watch fact sheets, available at hrw.org/english/docs/2006/01/18/pakist12254.htm and hrw.org/english/docs/2004/12/14/pakist9852.htm. the 7/21/04 BBC News article "Pakistan Army 'Killing Farmers'," available at news.bbc.co.uk/2/hi/south_asia/3915235.stm, and the 7/4/04 *Los Angeles Times* op-ed piece "As U.S. Talks of Liberty, Musharraf Scorns It" by Paula R. Newberg

Policy Review's Derek Chollet—in a review of Samantha Power's "The Problem from Hell: America and the Age of Genocide"—reported that George W. Bush was given a memo "summarizing" Power's chapter on the Rwanda genocide, which had been excerpted in *The Atlantic Monthly*. Bush wrote on the memo, "NOT ON MY WATCH." Save Darfur proceeded to sell bracelets with the four words to raise awareness of the Sudan genocide. *New York Times* columnist Nicholas Kristof has reminded Bush of his earlier statement in several columns, including "Why Should We Shield the Killers?" (2/2/05), "Facing Down the Killers" (12/18/04) and "Taking Bush at His Word" (10/30/04).

Information on the Bush Administration's efforts to renew ties with Sudan comes from the 4/29/05 *Los Angeles Times* article, "Official Pariah Sudan Valuable to America's War on Terrorism" by Ken Silverstein. *The American Prospect*'s Mark Leon Goldberg reported on how the Administration lowballed the Sudan death toll in a 4/29/05 online piece, "Zoellick's Appeasement Tour," available at www.prospect.org/web/page.ww?section=root&name=ViewWeb&articleId=9622. David Lepeska's United Press International piece, "Deepening Crisis In Darfur," ran on 2/9/06.

The Human Rights Watch report on the United Arab Emirates is available at hrw.org/english/docs/2006/01/18/uae12233.htm.

The BBC article about Equatorial Guinea's "oil star" status is available at news.bbc.co.uk/1/hi/business/2457763.stm. MSNBC.com reported on the Bush Administration's outreach to the dictatorship in Kari Huus's article "Bush Has Another Agenda in Africa," available at www.msnbc.com/news/934126.asp?0cv=CB10.

Secretary of State Condoleezza Rice's praise for the dictator of Equatorial Guinea can be found in the April 12, 2006 State Department release titled "Remarks With Equatorial Guinean President Teodoro Obiang Nguema Mbasogo Before Their Meeting."

Analysis of the Bush Administration's response to Egypt's sham election is available in the 12/16/05 *Washington Post* column "Beyond 'Democratic Peace'" by Susan E. Rice.

Background on lack of freedom in Jordan comes from Human Rights Watch's Overview, available at hrw.org/english/docs/2006/01/18/jordan12225.htm, *The Nation*'s 5/30/05 article "Letter From Jordan" by Stephen Glain, available at www.thenation.com/docprint.mhtml?i=20050530&s=glain, and the 3/16/05 Abu Aardvark blog post, "Jordan Bush Fails the Test," available at abuaardvark. typepad.com/abuaardvark/2005/03/jordan_bush_fai.html.
Details on the failed Venezuela coup can be found in 4/21/02 *The Observer* article "Venezuela Coup Linked to Bush Team" by Ed Vulliamy, available at observer. guardian.co.uk/international/story/0,6903,688071,00.html. Details on the successful Haiti coup can be found in Max Blumenthal's 1/30/06 Huffington Post article, "Uncovering A U.S.-Planned Coup in Haiti: The Original Version," available at www.huffingtonpost.com/max-blumenthal/uncovering-a-usplanned-c_b_14750.html, and the 1/29/06 *New York Times* article "Mixed U.S. Signals Helped Tilt Haiti Toward Chaos" by Walt Bogdanich and Jenny Nordberg.
The 7/5/04 *Boston Globe* article on the Middle East Partnership Initiative is "U.S. Reform Funds Take Different Path" by Farah Stockman.
The report "Integrated Power" was written by Lawrence J. Korb and Robert O. Boorstin and the National Security Staff of the Center For American Progress, published on 6/7/05 and available at www.americanprogress.org/site/pp.asp?c=biJRJ8OVF&b=742277.
Jeffrey Sachs laid out his plan to eradicate extreme poverty in the 3/14/05 *Time* magazine article "The End of Poverty." Sherle R. Schwenninger described his "New International Deal" in the essay "Reconnecting To the World," from the 7/18/05 issue of *The Nation*.
George Packer's 3/21/05 *New Yorker* article is "The Unbranding." Peter Beinart's essay on what he calls "post-Vietnam liberalism" is "A Fighting Faith," from the 12/13/04 *The New Republic*.

Chapter 5
Dr. D. James Kennedy quotes come from his book, *Character & Destiny: A Nation In Search of Its Soul*, compiled by Americans United for Separation of Church and State in the fact sheet, "They Said It! Religious Right Leaders In Their Own Words." Available at http://www.au.org/site/DocServer/They_Said_It.pdf.
Pat Buchanan's "culture war" speech to the 1992 Republican National Convention is available at www.buchanan.org/pa-92-0817-mc.html. CBS's Dick Meyer said, "Many mark [the Buchanan speech] as the official declaration of the culture war" in 7/22/04 online essay "The Official Start of Culture War," available at www.cbsnews.com/stories/2004/07/21/opinion/meyer/main631126.shtml.
Poll on gays in the military done by *USA Today*/CNN/Gallup between November 19 and 21, 2004, available at www.usatoday.com/news/polls/tables/live/2004-11-22-poll.htm.
2004 exit poll data on abortion and gay rights available at www.cnn.com/ELECTION/2004/pages/results/states/US/P/00/epolls.0.html.
Information about pre-2001 polls on gays in the military comes from the 8/6/01 press release by the Center for the Study of Sexual Minorities in the Military titled, "Polls Show Reduction of Soldiers' Opposition to Gays," available at www.gaymilitary.ucsb.edu/PressCenter/press_rel9.htm.
Poll data about the John Roberts and Sam Alito nominations comes from *Washington Post*–ABC surveys, available at www.washingtonpost.com/wp-dyn/content/custom/2005/12/20/CU2005122001059.html.

On the January 30, 2005, edition of NBC's *Meet the Press,* John Kerry confirmed a portion of a 12/20/04 *Newsweek* article, "Anxiety Over Abortion," which reported he told a group a liberal activists during a "closed-door confab" following the 2004 election that "they needed new ways to make people understand they didn't *like* abortion."

Howard Dean's abortion quote comes from a speech made to Utah Democrats, reported by the Associated Press's Paul Foy on 7/17/05, available at old. heraldextra.com/modules.php?op=modload&name=News&file=article&sid= 59907.

Senator Hillary Clinton's characterization of abortion as a "sad, even tragic choice" was made in a 1/24/05 speech to New York State family planning providers, transcript available at clinton.senate.gov/~clinton/speeches/2005125A05.html.

Background on medical reasons for late-term abortions comes from the National Abortion Federation fact sheet "Abortion After 12 Weeks." Fact sheet available at www.prochoice.org/about_abortion/facts/after_12_weeks.html.

The 7/3/05 *Washington Post Magazine* article that reported on Howard Dean's attempt to reframe the abortion message in Oklahoma is "Return of the Angry Man" by Sally Jenkins.

The ABC News poll showing support for the dilation and extraction late-term abortion procedure, when the health of the mother is at stake, was taken July 16 to 20, 2003. Data available at www.pollingreport.com/abortion.htm.

Joseph M. Scheidler, the national director of the Pro-Life Action League, told the *Boston Globe's* Stephanie Ebbert that "birth control is the kissing cousin of abortion" in the 10/15/05 article "Romney Signs Bill on Family Planning."

Pew Hispanic Center data on undocumented immigrants can found in the 3/21/05 report "Estimates of the Size and Characteristics of the Undocumented Population" and the 3/7/06 report "Size and Characteristics of the Unauthorized Migrant Population in the U.S.," both by Jeffrey S. Passel. Reports available at pewhispanic.org.

The source for the statistic on Americans illegally importing Canadian prescription drugs is David MacKay, executive director of the Canadian International Pharmacy Association, who was quoted in the 2/5/05 Canadian Press article "Internet Pharmacy Groups Mount Commons Offensive to Save Industry" by Michelle Macafee. The number was also cited in the 1/7/05 *Washington Post* article "Bush Accused of Influencing Canada on Drug Exports" by Doug Struck and the 5/13/05 *Las Vegas Review-Journal* article "Senators Waver on Drug Import Bill" by Ed Vogel.

Center for North American Studies (CNAS) director Robert Pastor's proposal for a North American Investment Fund is outlined in the 8/4/03 paper, "Closing the Development Gap: A Proposal for a North American Investment Fund," co-authored by Samuel Morley and Sherman Robinson of the International Food Policy Research Institute, available at the CNAS Web site, www.american.edu/ia/cnas. Pastor wrote a 3/8/06 *Miami Herald* op-ed, "Help Mexico, Lift All Boats" summarizing how the plan would curtail illegal immigration. Marcela Sanchez of washingtonpost.com promoted the plan in the 5/26/05 column, "Immigration Is Not the Only Problem," available at www.washingtonpost.com/wp-dyn/content/article/2004/05/28/AR2005033104207.html.

The March 22, 2006, poll by the Pew Research Center for the People and the Press on gay marriage is available at people-press.org/reports/display. php3?ReportID=273.

Gallup poll numbers on civil uniouns from 1996 and 2000 can be found at the Ontario Consultants on Religious Tolerance Web site, ReligiousTolerance.org.

Sen. Hillary Clinton's interview on CBS took place on 12/7/03 during the program *Face the Nation.*

Jonah Goldberg's criticism of Hillary Clinton was part of his 5/1/00 *National Review* article, "Why Not Gay Marriage?"

Information about SUV safety comes from the February 2005 *Consumer Reports* article "SUV Safety: Issues and Answers." Also worth reading is the 1/12/04 *New Yorker* article "Big and Bad" by Malcolm Gladwell.

Regarding data on light truck sales: A 1/16/01 report from the Congressional Research Service, "Sport Utility Vehicles, Mini-Vans and Light Trucks: An Overview of Fuel Economy and Emissions Standards" by Brent D. Yacobucci found, "in 1980, light trucks composed 19.9 percent of the U.S. new automobile market. By 1999, this figure had increased to 48.3 percent." In a 1/30/05 press release, the National Automobile Dealers Association reported, "In 2004, light trucks made up a record 55 percent of total light vehicles sales."

Information on how we're losing ground on fuel efficiency comes from the Sierra Club web page titled "Driving Up the Heat: SUVs and Global Warming" which includes the chart "Lowest Fleet Fuel Economy Average Since 1980," available at sierraclub.org/globalwarming/suvreport/energy.asp.

For background on new fuel efficiency rules implemented by the Bush Administration in March 2006, check out these two *Grist Magazine* online articles: "Go Truck Yourself," from 8/24/05 (no byline) at www.grist.org/news/daily/2005/08/24/1 and "Better Escalade than Never," from 3/30/06, by Amanda Griscom Little, at www.grist.org/news/muck/2006/03/30/fuel-economy.

The Yale poll on American attitudes toward the environment is an annual product of the Yale Center of Environmental Law and Policy's Environmental Attitudes and Behavior (EAB) Project. June 2005 survey data are available at www.yale.edu/envirocenter/environmentalpoll.htm.

Transcripts of the "Porn Rock" hearings—formally known as "Hearing Before the Committee on Commerce, Science, and Transportation, United States Senate, Ninety-Ninth Congress; First Session on Contents of Music and the Lyrics of Records"—which took place on 9/19/85, are available at http://mars.superlink.net/~jdandrea/shrg99-529/.

Chapter 6

Al and Tipper Gore quote comes from their book, *Joined at the Heart: The Transformation of the American Family.*

Public opinion about Terri Schiavo comes from an ABC News poll taken 3/20/05. ABC's Gary Langer analyzed the data in the 3/21/05 online article "Poll: No Role for Government in Schiavo Case," available at abcnews.go.com/Politics/PollVault/story?id=599622.

Pew Research Center for the People and the Press poll data on Democrats and religion are available in the 8/30/05 report "Religion a Strength and Weakness for Both Parties," available at people-press.org/reports/display.php3?ReportID=254.

Rev. Jim Wallis's comments come from his February 2004 article in *Sojourner* magazine, "The Democrats' Religion Problem."

The stat that 80 percent of Americans are Christian is an estimate based on the data in the Adherents.com article "Largest Religious Groups in the United States of America," which reported that a 2002 Pew Research Council survey found 82 percent are Christian, while the 2001 American Religious Identity Survey pegged the figure at 76.5 percent.

Poll data regarding the frequency with which voters attend religious services come from presidential election exit polls in 2000 and 2004, available at www.cnn.com/ELECTION/2000/epolls/US/P000.html and www.cnn.com/ELECTION/2004/pages/results/states/US/P/00/epolls.0.html, respectively.

Amy Sullivan's June 2003 *Washington Monthly* article is "Do the Democrats Have a Prayer?" The poll data she cited come from the 9/20/00 Pew Research Center for the People and the Press report "Religion and Politics: the Ambivalent Majority" available at people-press.org/reports/display.php3?ReportID=32.

The 2004 Pew data regarding separation of church and state was part of the 8/24/04 report "GOP the Religion-Friendly Party" available at people-press.org/reports/display.php3?ReportID=223.

Chapter 7

Michael Greve's quote comes from "The Unregulated Offensive" by Jeffrey Rosen in the 4/17/05 *New York Times Magazine.*

2004 exit poll data on abortion are available at www.cnn.com/ELECTION/2004/pages/results/states/US/P/00/epolls.0.html.

Lorraine Woellert's *Business Week* article is "Why Big Business Likes Alito," published on 11/1/05.

The New York Times's op-ed by Paul Gewirtz and Chad Golder ran on 7/6/05 and was titled "So Who Are the Activists?"

The "Gun Free School Zones" Supreme Court case is United States v. Lopez. The Violence Against Women Act Supreme Court case is United States v. Morrison.

The Cybercast News Service article featuring Wendy Wright was "Bill Would Reauthorize Violence Against Women Act" by Monisha Bansal, which was published on 6/10/05.

Statistics on domestic violence come from the February 2003 Bureau of Justice Statistics report "Intimate Partner Violence, 1993–2001" by Callie Marie Rennison.

Concerned Women for America (CWFA) praised John Roberts's opposition to the Violence Against Women Act in the 8/24/05 commentary "John Roberts: Women's Worst Nightmare?" by Janice Shaw Crouse, available at www.cwfa.org/articledisplay.asp?id=8780&department=BLI&categoryid=commentary.

CWFA promoted marriage as "the best protection" against domestic violence in the 6/12/03 commentary "The Violent Reality of Lovin' and Leavin'" by Kathryn Hooks, available at www.cwfa.org/articledisplay.asp?id=4107&department=BLI&categoryid=dotcommentary.

The U.S. District of Columbia Circuit Court of Appeals case involving John Roberts and endangered species is Rancho Viejo v. Norton. The U.S. Third Circuit Court of Appeals case involving Sam Alito and machine guns is U.S. v. Rybar.

The Cass Sunstein article is "Hoover's Court Rides Again" from the September 2004 *Washington Monthly.*

The 8/10/05 Oregonian article about Roberts and Sen. Ron Wyden is "Wyden Confident Roberts Would Shield Suicide Law" by Jim Barnett. The blog BlueOregon.com reminded readers about the article after Roberts voted to strike down the law.

Antonin Scalia's remarks at his confirmation hearing were reported by *The New York Times* on 8/6/86 in "Scalia Returns Soft Answers To Senators" by Stuart Taylor, Jr.

Clarence Thomas's remarks that he would have an "open mind" on Roe were noted in a 1/10/06 press release by the organization IndependentCourt.org titled "Alito 'Open Mind' on Roe Echoes Clarence Thomas Confirmation Hearing; Thomas Voted to Overturn Roe—What Would Alito Do?" His comments about past Supreme Court precedents were reprinted by Jan Crawford Greenberg in a June 2003 online forum for the Web site of PBS's *The NewsHour with Jim Lehrer,* accessed on 4/13/06 at www.pbs.org/newshour/forum/june03/scotus_forum2.html.

The 2001 Clean Water Act case involving William Rehnquist was Solid Waste Agency v. Army Corps of Engineers.

The 2003 family and medical leave case involving William Rehnquist was Hibbs v. Nevada Department of Human Resources. FoxNews.com's Jane Roh reported on Rehnquist's vote switch maneuver in that case for the 6/14/05 article "Rehnquist's Legacy: A Balanced Court" available at www.foxnews.com/story/0,2933,159308,00.html.

The 1/13/06 *Washington Post* article about the Alito confirmation was "Alito Likely to Become a Justice" by Charles Babington and Jo Becker.

The 1/12/06 *Chicago Tribune* article about the Alito confirmation was "Heat Turned Up, Alito Stays Cool" by Jill Zuckman and Jan Crawford Greenburg.

The CNN comments were made by Bob Franken and Miles O'Brien on *American Morning* and were included in a 1/11/06 Republican National Committee press release titled, "What They Are Saying about the Nomination Hearings of Judge Samuel Alito Jr.: Part V."

Chapter 8

Rush Limbaugh's entry in the online encyclopedia Wikipedia.org discusses how the repeal of the Fairness Doctrine freed "radio stations to air opinion journalism without having to provide air time to opposing points of view" and helped his career.

The difference between today's corporate media owners and yesterday's private press barons was described in the January/February 2006 *Columbia Journalism Review* article "A Way Out?" by Douglas McCollam.

The 10/23/02 Sidelines Online article about Al Gore's speech on the media is "Gore: 'News plus' drives network programming" by Patrick Chinnery.

The 10/2/03 Program on International Policy Attitudes study about Iraq news coverage is titled "Misperceptions, the Media and the Iraq War" and is available at www.pipa.org/online_reports.html.

National Public Radio audience size estimates come from the 3/28/05 *Billboard Radio Monitor* article "NPR Posts Listener Gains" by Tony Sanders. *New York Times* and PBS estimates come from their respective Web sites: www.nytimes.com/marketing/adinfo/home/faq.html and www.pbs.org/newshour/ww/history.html.

Donald Rumsfeld's 8/25/03 remarks on Iraq and the media were made in a speech to the Veterans of Foreign Wars in San Antonio. A transcript is available at www.defenselink.mil/speeches.

The 9/1/03 *National Review* article is "No Quagmire: How to Avoid One This Time" by John O'Sullivan. The 9/10/03 *Wall Street Journal* op-ed is "What Iraqis Really Think" by Karl Zinsmeister.

The history of antimedia e-mails about Iraq was detailed by Snopes.com at snopes.com/politics/war/combatend.asp.

The 8/15/05 *New York Times* article about how antimedia e-mails successfully pressured news outlets on Iraq coverage is "Editors Ponder How to Present a Broad Picture of Iraq" by Katharine Q. Seelye.

Keith Olbermann's blog, Bloggermann, is part of the MSNBC.com Web site. His posts about the e-mails he received in response to his election reporting were 11/9/04's "Electronic voting angst" and 11/21/04's "Relax about Ohio, Relax about the guy tailing me" available at www.msnbc.msn.com/id/6368819/#041109a and www.msnbc.msn.com/id/6533008/#041121a, respectively.

The NBC News memo about Phil Donahue was reported by Rick Eillis of AllYourTV.com in the 2/25/03 piece "The Surrender of MSNBC."

The ratings increase for *Countdown* was reported by the TVNewser blog, www.mediabistro.com/tvnewser, on 12/1/04.

The Washington Post's defense of a reporter facing criticism from liberals and conservatives was made in the introduction to a transcript of a 3/21/05 online chat with reporter Dana Milbank.

Background on the role of the blogs Eschaton and Talking Points Memo in the resignation of Trent Lott as Senate Majority Leader can be found in the 12/13/02 *New York Times* Paul Krugman column "The Other Face" and the 12/21/02 *Guardian* article by Oliver Burkeman, "Bloggers Catch What Washington Post Missed." To read the series of blog posts from Eschaton (atrios.blogspot.com) and Talking Points Memo (talkingpointsmemo.com), go to the archives section of each and find the posts from between 12/6/02 and 12/20/02.

The facts on Ruth Bader Ginsburg's Senate testimony on abortion rights are in the August 2005 American Constitution Society for Law and Policy report, "The Confirmation Hearings of Justice Ruth Bader Ginsburg: Answering Questions While Maintaining Judicial Impartiality" by Kristina Silja Bennard.

The facts about African-Americans and Social Security can be found in the March 2002 Social Security Network report "Setting the Record Straight: Two False Claims about African Americans and Social Security" by Bernard Wasow; the August 2003 AARP fact sheet "Social Security and African Americans: Some Facts" by Laurel Beedon and Ke Bin Wu; and the 4/22/99 Slate online magazine article "Race Bait and Switch" by Jodi Kantor.

While conservatives persist in accusing Ambassador Joe Wilson of lying for saying that Vice President Dick Cheney personally asked him to go to Niger in his 7/6/03 *New York Times* op-ed "What I Didn't Find in Africa," the op-ed itself disproves the charge. Wilson wrote, "I was informed by *officials at the Central Intelligence Agency* that Vice President Dick Cheney's office had questions about a particular intelligence report.... *The agency officials asked* if I would travel to Niger to check out the story so they could provide a response to the vice president's office." [emphasis added]

The Michael Gettler *Washington Post* ombudsman column is "A Stumble amid the Good Stuff" published on 9/11/05.

"A lie is halfway round the world before the truth has got its boots on" is a quote often falsely attributed to Mark Twain. It actually appears in the Oxford Dictionary of Proverbs.

Trudy Lieberman's January/February 2004 article in the *Columbia Journalism Review* is titled, "Answer the &$%#* Question!"

The quote from *New York Times* reporter Elisabeth Bumiller was reported in the 3/22/04 Baltimore Sun article, "Coaxing Straight Talk from Masters of Spin" by Alec MacGillis. It originated in the Spring 2004 installment of the White House Communication Series, a joint project of the University of California Washington Center and Towson University in which professors and students interview reporters and presidential aides about the White House relationship with the media. The Bumiller session is available at www.ucdc.edu/aboutus/whstreaming_2004.cfm.

Talking Points Memo criticized Bumiller's reporting on George W. Bush's response to Katrina in an untitled 9/2/05 post. A timeline of what did Bush after Katrina hit was compiled by the Think Progress blog at www.thinkprogress.org/katrina-timeline.

For more about Judith Miller's Iraq coverage at the *New York Times*, read Slate magazine's 4/23/03 "Follow That Story: Deep Miller" and 5/29/03 "Reassessing Miller," both by Jack Shafer, as well as Salon magazine's 5/27/04 "Not Fit to Print" by James C. Moore. For analysis of the *New York Times*'s "Editor's Note," read the 5/26/04 *Editor & Publisher* column "The New York Times, in 'Editors' Note,' Finds Much to Fault in Its Iraq WMD Coverage" by Greg Mitchell.

The 12/14/05 NPR ombudsman column is "NPR: Mysteries of the Organization, Part I" by Jeffrey A. Dvorkin, available at http://www.npr.org/templates/story/story.php?storyId=5053335

Jeffrey Rosen praised John Roberts on NPR during the 7/19/05, 9/5/05, and 9/13/05 editions of *All Things Considered*. Media Matters for America criticized NPR for pairing Rosen with a conservative supporter of Roberts in a 9/14/05 item, "*All* things considered? NPR host failed to mention that *TNR*'s 'liberal' Rosen endorsed Roberts for chief justice."

The 9/27/05 *Washington Post* article about conservative control of the Corporation for Public Broadcasting is "CPB Taps Two GOP Conservatives for Top Posts" by Paul Farhi.

Information about the ideological makeup of Rush Limbuagh's audience is from the 6/8/04 Pew Research Center for People and the Press report, "News Audiences Increasingly Politicized."

Information about Bill O'Reilly threatening callers who praised Olbermann comes from the Media Matters for America items "O'Reilly threatened radio show caller with 'a little visit' from 'Fox security' for mentioning Olbermann's name on the air" (3/3/06) and "Olbermann interviewed O'Reilly caller who was contacted by 'Fox News security'" (3/10/06), available at mediamatters.org.

Chapter 9

The March 2005 *Washington Monthly* article "Postmodern Protests" by Christina Larson discussed the importance of protests having strong messages and achieving tangible results.

Information about the March on Washington comes from the Web site for the book, *The Civil Rights Movement: A Photographic History 1954–68*, by Stephen Kasher (www.abbeville.com/civilrights/washington.asp); the transcript for the 4/14/03 Kennedy Library Forum featuring Representative John Lewis, the official program of the march downloaded at OurDocuments.gov; and the 9/16/03 press release from Representative Eddie Bernice Johnson "Remembering and Honoring the March on Washington of August 18, 1963," including the transcript of several U.S. House floor statements regarding a resolution in honor of the march.

David C. Ruffin's article in *Focus*, "We Stood Up at the March—A Memoir," appeared in the August 1998 edition.

Polls on civil rights from around the time of the March on Washington referenced here include the 7/14/63 "More Now Say Administration Pushing Integration 'Too Fast'" release from the American Institute of Public Opinion, and the 7/26/64 "Effects of Civil Rights Issue on Goldwater's Candidacy Assessed" article by George Gallup, director of the American Institute of Public Opinion.

Details on how the March 25, 2006 rally for immigrants came together were reported in the 3/28/06 *Los Angeles Times* article, "How DJs Put 500,000 Marchers in Motion" by Teresa Watanabe and Hector Becerra and the 3/28/06 *Washington Post* article, "Immigrants' Voice Reaches the Hill" by John Pomfret and Sonya Geis.

Seattle activist Geov Parrish criticized Eugene anarchists in his 12/8/99 *Seattle Weekly* column "Anarchists, go home!"

Jason Gay's 12/13/99 *Boston Phoenix* piece was titled, "Seattle Was a Riot."

Background on the March for Women's Lives comes from the 4/25/04 Women's eNews article, "Pro-Choice March Largest in History" by Allison Stevens, the May 2004 *Z Magazine* essay, "March for Women's Lives" by Eleanor J. Bader, and the 4/26/04 Salon magazine piece "Behind the scenes at the March for Women's Lives" by Rebecca Traister.

Complaints about media coverage of the March for Women's Lives were reported in "Media Play Was Light for Rally's Heavy Turnout" by Allison Stevens of Women's eNews on 5/6/04.

Regarding the Los Angeles student walkout, on 3/27/06 *Los Angeles Times* reporter Joel Rubin said on KCRW-FM that it was organized on MySpace.com. The comments were then relayed to the blog BoingBoing, in a post titled "LA student protests organized on MySpace."

Information about activism generated by DrinkingLiberally.org is from the 2/16/05 *Mother Jones* article "Promoting Democracy, One Pint at a Time" by Joel Gershon

Chapter 10

David Brock called the conservative network "the Republican noise machine" in his book with the same title. Robert Borosage called it "the mighty Wurlitzer" in a 5/6/02 *The American Prospect* essay with the same title.

Information on the "Wednesday meeting" comes from the 6/1/01 *USA Today* article, "Norquist's power high, profile low"

Grover Norquist's delightful farm animal metaphor was reported by *The Washington Post*'s "Reliable Source" column on 11/4/04.